Eisenhower and
Landrum-Griffin

EISENHOWER & LANDRUM-GRIFFIN

A Study in Labor-Management Politics

R. ALTON LEE

THE UNIVERSITY PRESS OF KENTUCKY

Copyright © 1990 by The University Press of Kentucky

Scholarly publisher for the Commonwealth,
serving Bellarmine College, Berea College, Centre
College of Kentucky, Eastern Kentucky University,
The Filson Club, Georgetown College, Kentucky
Historical Society, Kentucky State University,
Morehead State University, Murray State University,
Northern Kentucky University, Transylvania University,
University of Kentucky, University of Louisville,
and Western Kentucky University.

Editorial and Sales Offices: Lexington, Kentucky 40506-0336

Library of Congress Cataloging-in-Publication Data

Lee, R. Alton.
  Eisenhower and Landrum-Griffin : a study in labor-management
politics / R. Alton Lee.
     p.   cm.
  Includes bibliographical references.
  ISBN 0-8131-1683-X (alk. paper)
  1. United States. Labor-Management Reporting and Disclosure Act
of 1959. 2. Trade-unions—Law and legislation—United States.
3. Eisenhower, Dwight D. (Dwight David). 1890–1969. 4. United
States—Politics and government—1953–1961. I. Title.
KF3400.A32A165   1989
344.73'018'02632—dc20
[347.3041802632]   89–35961
                                                           CIP

Contents

Preface

Three major laws established a national labor policy in the twentieth-century United States. The first of these, the Wagner Act, was a part of the New Deal's efforts to assist the workingman during the Great Depression by encouraging the organization of unions. It listed unfair practices that management had been using to discourage unionization and required management to bargain collectively in good faith. It established the National Labor Relations Board to administer this policy, and members of the early NLRB interpreted their role as assisting workers in their organization efforts.

The second law was primarily a reaction to what were seen as excesses caused by the first. Unions flourished with swollen membership rolls in the succeeding organizational drives, a trend accelerated by the scarcity of labor during World War II. The reconversion period witnessed the usual wave of postwar strikes as workers sought to achieve wage gains to offset inflation and the loss of overtime they had enjoyed during the war. The public, denied consumer goods because of the strikes, was inflamed by newspaper headlines about the "uncontrolled power" of "irresponsible labor bosses" and turned against the strikers. The Eightieth Congress responded by passing the Taft-Hartley Act, which listed unfair practices unions could no longer pursue. From then on the National Labor Relations Board was supposed to be an impartial referee in labor-management strife. Twelve years later an angry Congress, again responding to the demands of an aroused public over the actions of powerful labor "bosses," enacted the

Landrum-Griffin bill, and, for the first time, the national government began to regulate the internal affairs of unions.

The conservative coalition of Republicans and southern Democrats in Congress played a significant role in revising the New Deal's national labor policy. Because of the nature of their constituents, these politicians found a common interest during the New Deal era in opposing the new economic and social programs of Franklin D. Roosevelt and the greatly expanded role of the national government. In regard to labor policy they were, if not exactly antiunion, at the very least supportive of legislation that would curtail union activities and the power of labor leaders. During the Truman-Eisenhower years, they constituted a majority in Congress and, when supported by public opinion, were able to enact these laws with large majorities.

Two principal developments led to the enactment of the Landrum-Griffin bill. The McClellan Committee exposed the infiltration of criminal elements into certain parts of the union movement in the postwar period and the subsequent increase in corruption and racketeering. These exposures convinced the public that labor bosses exerted too much power over their members and that too often these officials lived a life of luxury financed by the dues they forced their followers to pay. In addition, the Eisenhower administration successfully mobilized public opinion and the latent sentiment in Congress to clean out corruption in unions. When the House of Representatives approved the Landrum-Griffin Act, more congressmen were present and voting than on any other vote in the history of that legislative body.

For many years historians tended to follow the interpretation of John Kenneth Galbraith, who stigmatized the Eisenhower years as "the bland leading the bland." Recently, largely as a result of gaining access to important document collections from the Eisenhower administration, historians have significantly revised their evaluation of the achieve-

ments of his presidency and the caliber of his leadership.
Historians are discovering that he was a far better politician and leader than was previously believed. This investigation of the Landrum-Griffin Act is, at least in part, a
case study of the Eisenhower administration's formulation
of national labor policy. It reveals that in this area Dwight
D. Eisenhower was far from the dullard his detractors have
depicted for so many years. It also demonstrates that on
this issue he was not the "hidden-hand" president, as Fred
I. Greenstein has described him, but that he had a good
staff that performed very efficiently in mobilizing the necessary forces to gain passage of the law. Eisenhower's immense popularity was one of the assets the staff used to
solidify public opinion in support of Landrum-Griffin, and
he played his role very effectively to get the labor policy he
wanted.

The Eisenhower Library is a rich resource for the history
of his administration. The recently opened Ann Whitman
files contain a wealth of notes, memoirs, diary entries,
minutes of legislative meetings, and similar material that
many presidents would not keep for historians. I was disappointed in the paucity of helpful material in Secretary
James Mitchell's papers in Abilene but assumed I would
find more in his papers in the National Archives. There,
also, my expectations were not realized, and I was forced to
conclude that he did not play the key role one would expect from the secretary of labor in helping to get Eisenhower's labor reform law enacted, or if he did, he concealed the
evidence rather well.

The Senate papers of Lyndon Johnson were valuable, as
was the oral history of his aide for labor legislation, George
Reedy. While in Texas I also checked the Sam Rayburn Papers, which were sparse on materials on the Speaker's role
in the enactment of this labor legislation. When I mentioned this lack, compared to what I found in the Johnson
Library, the response of the library director, who had been

a Rayburn aide, was, "Mr. Sam did not operate the way Senator Johnson did." Apparently Rayburn conducted much of his business on this issue in person or by telephone and left little written record. Senator Dirksen's papers and the Kennedy Pre-Presidential File also contained little on the Landrum-Griffin Act, and Stephen Townsend of Indiana University reported that there was nothing of value on the Landrum-Griffin Act in the Charles Halleck Papers, deposited in the Lilley Library. Karl Mundt's rich collection of Senate papers was helpful on the Kohler strike hearings, as were the Walter Reuther Papers.

Phil Landrum very kindly responded to questions about his role in this legislation, and Robert Griffin generously gave me several hours of his time to discuss his law. His counsel for the Republicans on the House Committee on Education and Labor, Kenneth McGuiness, talked to me one morning by telephone, discussing his recollections about the legislation. Senator Barry Goldwater kindly responded to questions about the conference committee work. Finally, I talked at length with Edward McCabe, the White House liaison for labor legislation, about the administration's role in the passage of the Landrum-Griffin Act. I thank these busy gentlemen for sharing their insights and knowledge, which made this a better work.

Alan McAdam's book *Power and Politics in Labor Legislation* began as a doctoral dissertation in political science. He interviewed many of the participants during or immediately after the enactment of the law, and I consider his book to be a primary source. So, too, are the books about the McClellan Committee investigations written by those who participated in the hearings on corruption in labor unions or were reporters helping to uncover the story.

In pursuing this study I received a great deal of assistance, both financially and through the services of archivists, librarians, and colleagues. The National Endowment for the Humanities awarded me a travel grant to do research at the Dwight D. Eisenhower Library. The Lyndon

Baines Johnson Foundation gave me an award to travel to that library. Howard Coker and the University of South Dakota Office of Research have been most supportive of my research and helped finance trips to interview participants on two occasions, and the General Research Fund of the University of South Dakota made it possible for me to visit the National Archives. A grant from the Walter P. Reuther Library helped defray expenses for a research trip to Wayne State University. The James and Ruth Ann Weaver Fund helped support publication expenditures.

The following librarians and archivists were most generous with their time and assistance: John Wickman, Herb Pankratz, and Dwight Strandberg of the Dwight D. Eisenhower Library; Saundra Taylor of the Lilly Library, Indiana University; Janet M. Lange and Frank Mackaman of the Everett Dirksen Congressional Center; Jerry Hess of the National Archives; Judson MacLaury, historian for the Department of Labor; H.G. Dulaney of the Sam Rayburn Library; Claudia Johnson of the Lyndon Baines Johnson Library; Pearl Hefte of the Karl Mundt Archives; Philip P. Mason and Warner W. Phlug of the Walter P. Reuther Library; Jane B. Ward of the John Fitzgerald Kennedy Library; and Jim Beasley, Miriam Kahn, Max Leget, David Olson, and John Van Balen of the University of South Dakota's I.D. Weeks Library.

Finally, I would like to thank Professors Robert Hilderbrand and Gerald Wolff of the University of South Dakota and Professor William Howard Moore of the University of Wyoming for reading the manuscript. Each, in his own way, made suggestions for improving it in many ways. Although I did not always accept their suggestions, they forced me to rethink what I had written, and this book is better for their help. I must accept responsibility, of course, for any errors or weaknesses that remain.

1. Unions and the Democrats

It is a truism that labor unions thrive on adversity, and seldom in American history did they face greater affliction than during the Great Depression. As the economic spiral continued downward during the 1930s, desperate workers turned increasingly to the American Federation of Labor (AFL) for union charters in hopes of bettering their lot through organization and collective bargaining. In turn, President Franklin D. Roosevelt and his New Deal administration decided these efforts needed encouragement and assistance and persuaded Congress to establish a national labor policy that promoted the growth of unions.

In an effort to stimulate industrial recovery, the first New Deal enacted the National Industrial Recovery Act of 1933, which established the National Recovery Administration (NRA). Section 7(a) of this law for the first time gave federal sanction for workers to organize and be represented by a collective bargaining agent as guaranteed by the "codes of fair competition" provided in the law. But the law was quickly challenged, and two years later in *Schechter* v. *U.S.* (the "Sick Chicken" case) the Supreme Court declared the NRA unconstitutional. Senator Robert Wagner, Democrat from New York, who authored much of the most important New Deal labor legislation, revived Section 7(a) and expanded it into the National Labor Relations Act, commonly called the Wagner Act, which Congress approved in 1935.

The Wagner Act again brought the national government into the collective bargaining process on the side of laborers. The purpose of the new labor policy, as stated in the preamble to the act, was "to eliminate the causes of certain substantial obstructions to the free flow of commerce . . . by encouraging the practice and procedure of collective organizing and by protecting the exercise of workers of full freedom of association, self-organization, and designation of representatives of their own choosing, for the purpose of negotiating the terms and conditions of their employment or other mutual aid or protection."[1] The law listed unfair labor practices that management had pursued in the past to restrict unionism, required employers to bargain with unions in good faith, and established a three-man National Labor Relations Board (NLRB) to administer the policy and help workers organize unions.

This new labor policy, one of the cornerstones of the New Deal's attempts to help workers recover economically, fostered a political alliance between labor leaders and the Democratic party. The New Deal staffed the NLRB with prolabor members who believed it was their duty to help unions and workers in labor-management conflicts, and union leaders in turn supported the Democratic party. The teamsters and the building trades unions that continued to support the Republican party during the postwar period were curious exceptions to this pattern.

The Supreme Court held the Wagner Act to be constitutional in *NLRB* v. *Jones and Laughlin Steel* (301 U.S. 1) in 1937 but two years later dealt a body blow to the fundamental right to strike. In *NLRB* v. *Mackay Radio & Telegraph* (304 U.S. 333) the court held that it was not an unfair labor practice for an employer to replace striking workers on the grounds that the employer has the right "to protect and continue his business." This decision, one labor law expert declared, "drastically undercut the new act's protection of the critical right to strike." If the employer did not commit any unfair labor practice, employees had no right to automatic reinstatement after the strike was settled.[2]

Despite this legal setback, union membership doubled during the next few years and the union leadership split. The AFL had been dominated for decades by the philosophy of Samuel Gompers and William Green, who argued that unions should concentrate on organizing craft workers to the neglect of those employed in mass production. A number of presidents of AFL-affiliates, led by John L. Lewis of the United Mine Workers (UMW), disagreed with this position and broke away to form the Congress of Industrial Organizations (CIO) in 1937, with the intent of organizing workers in the mass industries. The AFL soon decided it was a mistake to oppose organizing unskilled workers and joined in a race with the CIO to recruit members from any work category, with the result that occasionally violent jurisdictional conflicts occurred between the two. The AFL also decided that the NLRB favored the CIO in these jurisdictional disputes and sought changes in, and some AFL leaders advocated repeal of, the Wagner Act.[3]

Conversion to war production brought further increases in union membership—up to a total of 15 million from a 1932 low of under 3 million. The war also brought changes in the negotiating process. The Office of Price Administration froze prices and wages so unions were reduced to negotiating for little more than job security and fringe benefits for their members, which became substitutes for wage increases. The National War Labor Board allowed maintenance-of-membership clauses (these gave workers fifteen days to leave a union if they wished to do so; after that they had to remain members for the duration of the contract), and many unions forced management to grant job security, profit sharing, health and insurance programs, and similar fringe benefits. Most government contracts were negotiated on a cost-plus basis so management had no difficulty in passing these increased costs on to the American taxpayer.[4]

At the end of the war, labor-management conflict escalated. Laborers in the reconversion period feared the typical postwar increase in unemployment, and they also wanted to keep their wartime gains in wages. In converting to peacetime production, however, management no longer had the cost-plus outlet to absorb increased costs and sought to keep high wartime profits by denying wage increases. The result was a series of devastating strikes in late 1945 and 1946 with almost 5 million workers involved in 4,630 work stoppages in one year. The strikes created an increasingly hostile public reaction against unions and labor leaders, whom management and the mass media successfully blamed for the strife. Union leaders were viewed as exercising "uncontrollable power."

Centralization of authority in unions was one of the noticeable trends in the postwar period. Power shifted from the shop floor, where it had traditionally resided in the previous half-century, to the union bureaucracy, and in most unions authority was concentrated in the hands of the top executives.[5] Thus in the reconversion period the media successfully portrayed John L. Lewis and other union leaders as arrogant union bosses whose power needed to be controlled.

Industrial organizations like the United States Chamber of Commerce and the National Association of Manufacturers (NAM), which had opposed the Wagner Act since its inception, continued to work for its repeal. Following World War II, management decided that the powerful trade union movement that developed during the 1930s was there to stay and must be controlled and the participation of union leaders in management decisions forestalled. In the reconversion period, management organizations conducted a massive campaign to convince the public that labor leaders had become irresponsible and union power should be curbed. The nation's mass media joined in this effort, presenting the series of nationwide strikes as the natural result of unions gaining too much power under the Wagner

Act. When John L. Lewis called a strike of his miners in 1946, citizens focused their attention on one man whom the media was labeling "irresponsible." The public, frustrated with postwar shortages of consumer goods and desiring products they believed were being denied them by the greed of union workers, agreed that the unfettered power of union leaders should be curtailed. The conservative coalition in Congress was able to exploit this public frustration to its advantages.

The conservative coalition was, and is, an informal alliance of conservative Republicans and southern Democrats with common interests on various domestic policy issues. These improbable allies discovered in the 1930s that they were in agreement in opposing the expanding social and economic policies of the second New Deal, the deficit spending and unbalanced budgets required to fund the depression programs, and the northern Democrats' philosophy of "tax and tax, spend and spend, and elect and elect." Conservative Republicans found that if they joined southern Democrats in opposing civil rights legislation, southern congressmen often would support their opposition to further expansion of the New Deal. The conservative coalition was flexible, informal, and did not always include the same members on any given issue, but it was real and particularly after the election of 1936 was a growing, viable alliance in Congress.[6] Using the issue of strikes and irresponsible labor leaders, members of the conservative coalition sought and believed they received a mandate from the voters in the election of 1946 to curb union power.

The Eightieth Congress, which convened in January 1947, was controlled by the Republicans for the first time since 1930. Joined by their southern Democratic allies, they pressed the Taft-Hartley Act through Congress and passed it over the veto of President Harry S. Truman. This legislation amended the Wagner Act, which was the only New Deal program to be significantly altered or reversed in the postwar era.[7] The Hartley bill in the House was much

more harsh on union practices than the Taft bill in the
Senate, and in the conference committee Taft won on most
of the disputed issues.

The Labor-Management Relations Act of 1947 (Taft-
Hartley) made several important changes in the Wagner
Act. Based on the premise that the national government
should be an impartial referee rather than a union supporter in labor-management conflict, the law listed a series
of unfair labor practices now forbidden to unions. The purpose of the Taft-Hartley Act, according to its supporters,
was to draw up a fair balance sheet, and the NLRB should
not be a partisan of either side in labor-management issues.
An addition to the Wagner Act preamble was inserted in
its preamble: "Experience has further demonstrated that
certain practices by some organizations, their officers, and
members, have the intent or necessary effect of burdening
or obstructing commerce by preventing the free flow of
goods in such commerce through strikes or other forms of
industrial unrest or through concerted activities which
impair the interest of the public in the free flow of such
commerce. The elimination of such practices is a necessary condition to the assurance of the rights herein
guaranteed."[8]

Union leaders loudly and bitterly denounced the Taft-
Hartley Act as a "slave labor law" and insisted that President Truman veto it. After studying the bill thoroughly
and receiving advice from all sides, Truman decided that,
although the law was a good one, he should veto it for political reasons. As he explained to James J. Reynolds, a
member of the NLRB: "Everybody thinks I am pro-labor,
and I am—but they've [labor leaders] gone too far in many,
many ways. I'm convinced Taft-Hartley is a pretty good
law. I've had a head count made on the Hill, and I know
that if I veto it my veto's going to be overridden. So we're
going to have a pretty good law on the books in spite of my
veto, and if I veto it, I'm going to have labor support in the
election next year."[9] Truman was right on all counts. His

veto was overridden and unions remained in the Democratic fold, becoming more active politically than ever before and helping Truman to be elected president in his great upset victory in 1948. He was also correct in his judgment that Taft-Hartley was a "pretty good law"; although it has not worked the way Representative Fred Hartley had hoped, union leaders have learned to live with its restrictions. Truman got to have his cake and eat it too. He received the political benefits of opposing the law and also was able to invoke the Taft-Hartley injunction procedure on several occasions during his presidency. The passage of the act gave management a big boost in its climb back to wielding the political and social influence it had lost during the Great Depression. Enactment of the Labor-Management Relations Act seemed to indicate that the social and political revolutions of the New Deal ideology had finally burned out.

The post–World War II era brought other major changes for organized labor in the United States. Section 14(b) of the Taft-Hartley Act allowed states to enact laws forbidding mandatory union membership; during the following decade nineteen states, mostly agrarian ones in the South and West, enacted right-to-work, or as unions dubbed them "right-to-wreck," statutes. These laws stimulated the decentralization of production facilities and their relocation into the low-wage, union-free Sunbelt states that had an antiunion local culture. In the postwar era the CIO launched a drive called Operation Dixie to unionize the South. Management successfully opposed this effort by taking advantage of antiunion sentiment in the South and by securing the assistance of conservative judges, who issued injunctions and rulings that helped manufacturers delay and resist NLRB rulings. The success of the J.P. Stevens Company in fending off unionism since 1963 illustrates how employers who are willing to spend money can thwart the intent of the national labor policy.

In addition, the years after 1945 witnessed the introduc-

tion of new technologies that weakened strongly organized, strategically located work groups and also brought
about the exporting of that technology abroad. American
industry began diversifying into disconnected industries
whose workers had no bargaining alliances and establishing overseas operations to take advantage of low wage
bases of Third World nations. All these developments reduced management's vulnerability to the union pressures
that had resulted in the massive organization of workers in
the 1930s and 1940s.[10]

Inflation, too, played a role in labor-management relations. In the automobile strikes of 1946, United Automobile Workers (UAW) president Walter Reuther demanded a
pay raise that would come from what he called the exor-
bitantly high profits of manufacturers. When management
responded that profits were low and wage increases would
have to come from price increases, Reuther demanded the
unthinkable—he asked management to make its books
public and reveal its profit levels. An aghast management
adamantly refused, and the strikes were settled by increasing wages and prices. If Reuther had won his point and that
settlement had served as a model, wage gains in the postwar period would have come from profits, not price increases. Management won the principle, however, and the
result was a spiral of inflation; each wage gain caused a rise
in consumer prices.[11] This trend proved to be a most significant development in postwar American society and
economy.

In 1948 the UAW signed a precedent-setting contract
with General Motors. During the postwar era, auto workers labored under the constant threat of seasonal layoffs.
Their financial insecurity was compounded by the widespread practice of installment buying of such items as
homes, vehicles, and appliances. The union solution was a
contract with cost-of-living escalator clauses (COLAs), an
idea that quickly spread to their negotiations with other
automakers and then to other types of industry. From this

point on, management was willing to offer COLAs, increased health care, retirement benefits, and paid vacations and holidays in return for the stability of long-term contracts. These added benefits for workers, of course, contributed to the inflationary spiral. But the long-term contracts, union security, and the direct checkoff of union dues by the employer all gave union leaders a greater vested interest in developing harmonious relations with management. Union leaders, in other words, were willing to sacrifice a role in management decision making for the sake of economic security for their members and themselves. As a result, the decade of the 1950s brought considerable affluence to union workers, as was visible in their increased movement to the suburbs (half of all workers in 1966), home and car ownership, installment buying, and wives working outside the home. Walter Reuther noted that "the labor movement . . . [developed] a whole new middle class."[12]

Two significant changes in the postwar labor force also affected organized labor. First, a surge in the growth of white-collar workers brought a major change in the occupational structure of the American work force. In the first decade and a half after 1945, white-collar employment constituted 75 percent of the increase in nonfarm labor. As a result, by 1960 there were more white-collar workers than production workers in the labor force. Second, women remained an important part of the work force after World War II. In that same fifteen-year period the number of women laborers increased about 40 percent. When the Taft-Hartley Act was passed, they constituted about 28 percent of nonfarm labor; when John F. Kennedy became president, they accounted for about one-third of all civilian laborers. White-collar workers and women never demonstrated particular interest in joining labor unions, which meant that the largest and most rapidly growing segments of the labor force in the post-Taft-Hartley period were resistant to unionization. The 1960s saw a reversal in this trend with "a remarkable trade-union penetration of the rapidly growing public sector." At the beginning of the decade, one in ten public employees was a union member; at the end of the decade the number had jumped to one in two. In addition, there was significant union recruitment of workers in hospitals, agriculture, food processing, and southern textile factories. The American Federation of Labor, the American Federation of Government Employees, the American Federation of State, County and Municipal Workers, the National Education Association, and the American Nurses Association were then numbered among the giants of organized labor. By 1980 one in four nonfarm workers was organized compared to one in three in 1945, but one-fourth of these, or over 5 million, were white-collar employees.[13]

Although the union-shop principle and maintenance of membership rules brought a surge in union membership during the war and postwar years, these new members often had little understanding of, and gave little support to, the concepts of unionism. Rather than being organized and indoctrinated, millions of workers had become unionized by a decree from Washington. They were often alienated from their leaders on issues concerning the purposes and functions of their union. They had their union dues checked off, and these contributions swelled welfare and pension funds. A few labor leaders proved unable to handle the temptation presented by these enormous funds entrusted to their care for investment, and some portions of the labor movement became involved in racketeering. In many cases, as the McClellan Committee hearings would demonstrate, state and local governments were unwilling or unable to cope with this unchecked corruption and racketeering and the American public had a new labor villain—union presidents who were criminals.[14] The ultimate result was a congressional effort to control this corruption through the Landrum-Griffin Act.

During the postwar period, management changed its bureaucratic control over decision making by developing

"company policy," or work rules. The new policy con-
sisted of the definition and direction of work tasks, the
evaluation of work performance, and the distribution of re-
wards and imposition of punishments according to stated
company policy. This significant change had at least two
major results in the workplace: foremen could no longer
evaluate performances capriciously, and work rules or
company policy became another important bargaining issue. This altered bureaucratic control invited political
struggles to change the rules. As one authority has noted,
"Increasingly, the working class has turned away from
unions and looked instead to government to regulate, protect, and provide. Unions continue to be important in this
process, but their role has changed; more and more what is
important is their political strength and not their industrial puissance."[15]

Organized labor also became directly entangled in the
Cold War that emerged after 1945. As Harry Truman developed his policy of containment of communism—a policy continued by his successor, Dwight D. Eisenhower—
he attempted to win the support of organized labor for this
bipartisan foreign policy. Communists within the CIO led
the fight to oppose Truman's plan to rebuild Western European economies and to integrate the West's military
forces to oppose the menace of communism. The Taft-Hartley Act aided immeasurably in this anticommunist struggle. Walter Reuther and his supporters defeated communist
leadership in many CIO affiliates by using the Taft-Hartley
requirement that union officials sign a noncommunist affidavit or lose NLRB benefits.[16]

In 1948 the CIO endorsed support for the United Nations, condemned Russia's extensive use of the veto power
in the Security Council, and approved the Marshall Plan to
rebuild Western Europe's economies. At its 1949 convention the CIO further amended its constitution to prohibit
communists from holding office in the union and to expel the remaining communist-led affiliates of which the

United Electrical Workers was the largest. These acts brought the CIO in line with AFL policies.[17]

In addition, organized labor leaders became active Cold Warriors, assisting the Central Intelligence Agency (CIA) in its covert fight against communism in Europe. Communist dock workers in West European countries, especially France, Italy, and West Germany, were attempting to sabotage the Marshall Plan by blocking the unloading of American goods. The CIA needed help in subverting these communist efforts and eventually found the right man in Jay Lovestone. Once chief of the Communist party, USA, Lovestone became one of the most effective leaders of the anticommunist movement in Western Europe during the Cold War. As an assistant to David Dubinsky, president of the International Ladies Garment Workers Union, Lovestone and his aide, Irving Brown, organized a successful anticommunist union in France, the Force Ouvrier. When they ran out of funds, they approached the CIA for money. Thomas Braden, an assistant to Allen W. Dulles, deputy director of the CIA, persuaded his boss that the agency should take the offensive in fighting communism through covert operations and began funding Brown and Lovestone in their anticommunist activities. The CIA also funded a number of the AFL's anticommunist ventures. When Walter Reuther complained that the AFL was receiving CIA funding and the CIO was not, Braden gave him $50,000 in $50 bills to help finance his anticommunist activities in Germany, although Braden did not think Reuther used the money very effectively.[18]

On the domestic scene, in 1945 organized labor's power appeared to be awesome and irresistible. But in the following years that power began to decline. In addition, the concerns of organized labor expanded to include a broader range of social issues than those of the depression and war years. It was no longer sufficient to "reward labor's friends and punish labor's enemies" at the ballot box. In Detroit in the 1940s, for example, the UAW supported blacks on the issues of housing and police brutality and, as David Brody puts it, "forged a durable political alliance with a black community hitherto distrustful of the labor movement." Union leaders were included among the founding fathers of the Americans for Democratic Action, a liberal political movement of the postwar era. Both the CIO and AFL became more concerned with the cause of the common man on social as well as economic issues. In fact, the AFL-CIO proved to be "a better champion of the general welfare than of its own narrow interests." This situation may have been more a matter of necessity than choice, as demonstrated in 1959, when union leaders "exchanged the tone of high-minded social advocacy for an unyielding, often strident opposition" to union reform—and the result was the Landrum-Griffin Act.[19]

During the postwar era labor leaders continued to make the Taft-Hartley Act a political issue by insisting on abolishing it and later, after repeated failures, by working to remove its most objectionable features. Following Truman's surprising victory in 1948, his administration and labor leaders pressed unsuccessfully for repeal of the law. The conservative coalition, led by Robert A. Taft and John Wood, Democrat from Georgia, contained a majority that refused to abolish Taft-Hartley. The only change came in 1951, when Congress eliminated the union-shop election provision because it was useless. Over 85 percent of the workers involved in these elections had supported the union-shop concept, and Congress decided they could dispense with expensive elections. Unions also failed in their attempt to purge their great enemy, Republican Robert Taft of Ohio, in his senatorial campaign of 1950. Resisting organized labor's all-out campaign against him, Taft successfully appealed to the rank-and-file workers for their vote and won. This election demonstrated vividly that labor leaders could not always deliver the labor vote to the candidates they endorsed. Taft continued to oppose labor's demands for repeal of his law although he would agree to some changes during the next three years.

Following Taft's return to the Eighty-second Congress,

union tactics shifted from insistence on outright repeal to
urging changes to abolish the most undesirable features of
Taft-Hartley, and "management groups in certain industries began to support labor demands for particular amendments." Also, certain unions began to seek modifications
that were advantageous to themselves. In 1951 the Senate
debated a bill that would legalize maritime hiring halls.
Both the longshoremen's union and the Pacific Maritime
Association supported this idea, but Senator Taft opposed
it on the grounds that the Taft-Hartley Act made a closed-
shop hiring hall illegal and did not include the maritime
hiring hall so it was not needed. With his powerful opposition, the Senate recessed without taking a vote on the
bill. Also in 1951 the AFL's building and construction
trades union sought to legalize a union shop in that industry. The United Mine Workers opposed this, as did the machinists union, because it would virtually eliminate them
from the construction industry. The lack of labor unity
killed any chances for the legislation, and it died in committee.[20] Union leaders then looked to the election of 1952
to achieve their goal of either eliminating Taft-Hartley or
amending away its most damaging provisions.

Despite union efforts to make the Taft-Hartley Act an
issue in the election of 1952, other political disputes
proved to be more important. The Republican platform
that year contained a plank that vaguely called for changes
in the law to ensure "industrial peace." When the Republican candidate, Dwight Eisenhower, was asked his views
on use of the Taft-Hartley labor injunction, he responded
that he did not know enough about the subject to venture
an opinion. During his campaign Eisenhower expressed the
view that it was impossible to "compel people to work.
That is regimentation. We have got to find a way, a means
of respecting the advances labor has made. I believe we
should not give up those social gains." When he addressed
the annual AFL convention, the Republican candidate informed the delegates that he opposed repeal of Taft-Hartley

but favored an amendment to eliminate the provision that "could be used to smash unions." Eisenhower supporters, when asked what he meant, said they believed he was referring to the restriction that economic strikers (striking over economic issues as opposed to grievance issues) could not vote in a representation election. Eisenhower also recalled for the AFL delegates that when Truman asked Congress to draft railroad strikers in 1946, the president called him as chief of staff to inform him of his plans. Eisenhower told Truman that if the strikers were drafted he would resign rather than take command over them.

His Democratic opponent, Adlai E. Stevenson, perhaps had an even greater problem with labor policy—he disagreed completely with his party's platform on the Taft-Hartley Act. In the pre-convention skirmishing for delegates, Stevenson had advocated necessary revisions in the labor law. But the Democratic platform, as written by Truman and his supporters, called for outright repeal because the Taft-Hartley Act had proven to be "inadequate, unworkable, and unfair." The platform declared that the entire labor-management problem should be thoroughly examined and a new labor policy written on the basis of that study. After his nomination, Stevenson refused to retreat from his earlier opposition to repeal, and later in the campaign he enunciated some basic principles that he would follow when writing a new labor law.

Despite Stevenson's ambivalent position on labor policy, most union leaders endorsed his candidacy. Truman hit the hustings as he had done in 1948, trying to excite union members about the "slave labor law," but to no avail. Eisenhower defeated Stevenson handily. The Taft-Hartley Act was not the critical issue in 1952 that Truman had made it in 1948; in fact, the law played little part in the outcome of the election. Voters turned out in record numbers to elect their hero president on the basis of such issues as the Korean War and Truman's "mess in Washington," as Republicans described the recent revelations of corruption

in government, and the issue of communists in government.[21] Union leaders then worried about what, if anything, the Republicans, who had been out of the White
House for two decades, would do to alter the national labor
policy.

Enough Republicans rode to victory on Eisenhower's
coattails that they gained control of the Eighty-second
Congress, but his popularity could not carry them further.
The Democrats captured a majority in Congress in the
midterm elections of 1954 and retained control for the remainder of Eisenhower's presidency. In the elections of
1958 the Democrats gained the greatest majorities in Congress since the Roosevelt landslide of 1936. During his
last six years in office, Eisenhower had to work with the
Democratic leadership to get his program approved and
during his last two years had to wield the veto power on
many occasions.

The Eisenhower years were far more business-oriented
than the New Deal and Fair Deal had been. Businessmen
and industrialists wielded much more influence during the
1950s and union leaders far less on the national government, a significant reversal of the previous twelve years.
And though organized labor held conflicting views on how
to revise the national labor policy, management was basically in accord that the Taft-Hartley Act needed to be
"toughened up." Management was greatly helped by the
often criminal behavior of a few irresponsible union officials in obtaining the desired revisions in the labor laws.
They were also significantly assisted by the promanagement views of the Eisenhower administration.

The AFL and the CIO differed sharply over many of the
provisions of the Taft-Hartley Act. The CIO listed several
items it said it wanted deleted but wisely did not press any
issue for fear that if Congress began making changes, they
might be more stringent than the original provisions of the
act. The building trades unions in the AFL, however, were
especially incensed over the loss of their hiring halls and

were operating them sub rosa, working ceaselessly for their legal restoration. The AFL was forced to support its affiliates because of the fear that the skilled crafts would invade its jurisdiction.[22]

Organized labor was split over both philosophy and goals during the postwar period, a time when practical politics called for it to present a united front. Some of these differences dated from the great division in the 1930s and would continue long after the merger of the two internationals in 1955, even though that merger was sparked primarily by the need for unity for political purposes. The AFL was composed of both craft unions that advocated practices necessitated by their specific skills and workers in mass production industries who pursued different goals. These divisions were often so strong that the AFL executive council was forced into ambivalence on labor issues. The CIO also was composed of various affiliated unions, but it was dominated by the philosophy of Walter Reuther and his United Auto Workers, its largest affiliate. Much of its divisiveness ended with the expulsion of the communist-dominated affiliates during the Cold War, although David McDonald and his influential United Steel Workers were restive over the UAW's dominance of the CIO. Thus, although the international officers of the AFL and the CIO seldom worked at cross-purposes on labor legislation, their affiliates and even members of their executive councils often supported opposing and selfish programs and political activities, even after the merger that created the AFL-CIO. This divisiveness would result not only in failure to secure desired changes in Taft-Hartley but would permit passage of labor legislation opposed by all unions and union leaders.

2. Unions and
   the Republicans

When the American people elected Dwight Eisenhower president in 1952 and gave the Republicans control of Congress for only the second time since 1930, many union leaders knew it was unrealistic to expect repeal of the Taft-Hartley Act. Officially, the CIO continued to insist on repeal, but the AFL decided to work for amendments that would remove features that adversely affected some AFL affiliates. Union leaders were uncertain which changes the new president would support because almost nothing was known about his attitude toward unions except that he was a Republican and therefore would probably be supportive of management. Labor policy was not a major issue in the campaign of 1952, and candidate Eisenhower had only occasionally expressed his views on the subject. As events unfolded during his first year in office, his secretary of commerce, Sinclair Weeks, began to play a dominant role in domestic issues and proved to be more influential in determining the administration's labor policy than the secretary of labor. Weeks was adamant that any changes in Taft-Hartley must strengthen, not weaken, the labor-management policy, and he succeeded in moving the Eisenhower administration in that direction.

President Eisenhower was never really comfortable around union leaders, especially when they did not play the role he expected of them. Although he had a laboring class background, it was rural, and he had spent his entire adult life in the military, except for a brief stint as presi-

dent of Columbia University. He found it difficult to relate
to union problems, policies, and philosophy. He proved
much more willing to understand and respond to the interests of the wealthy businessmen he became acquainted
with in the postwar period. His fundamental attitude toward unions surfaced, probably unconsciously, at the time
he and his wife, Mamie, were building their Gettysburg
house in 1954. He was disturbed by the basic union precept
that when one union on a job strikes, the other unions on
the project also walk out. Eisenhower confided to his secretary that this rule cost him an extra $65,000 to construct
his house and, "consequently he feels fairly strongly about
it."[1]

As Robert Griffith has carefully demonstrated, Eisenhower's basic philosophy for modern America entailed a
"corporate commonwealth," a need to create a harmonious society free of class conflict, unchecked greed, and de-
structive partisanship. He was particularly annoyed with
the waves of postwar strikes and what he considered to be
the resulting contentious party politics. He therefore appointed cabinet members who he believed shared his philosophy, and he expected all of the secretaries to work as a
team toward this goal. As Robert Gray, secretary to the
cabinet, put it, "Eisenhower used his Cabinet as a nonvot-
ing board of directors before which developing executive
problems and future plans were presented." Eisenhower accepted Social Security and other New Deal innovations as
necessary, and he conceded that unions were a vital part of
the corporate structure, but he was concerned over what
he considered their appeal to class consciousness and their
selfishness that could lead to disastrous inflation. Labor
must cooperate and strive for the common good of the corporate commonwealth. He held the altruistic notion that
both unions and management groups must subsume their
special interests and serve the public interest of the commonwealth. The secretary of labor must be a part of his
team to promote this ideal. Thus in the first six months of

his administration, Eisenhower cooperated with Senator
Robert Taft in trying an accommodationist approach to organized labor; the two tried to develop a number of amendments that would remove or mitigate the most pernicious
provisions of Taft-Hartley.[2]

Eisenhower believed organized labor should be represented in his cabinet to help contribute to the goal of the
corporate commonwealth, so he appointed Martin P. Durkin, head of the plumbers union and former head of the Illinois Department of Labor, as his secretary of labor. The
AFL, of course, was pleased with his choice and encouraged that one of its leaders was selected, but Taft was
stunned. He was not consulted about the nomination, but
if he had been he would have suggested "either the moderate John Danaker, a former Senate colleague from Connecticut, or the very conservative Clarence Manion, dean
of the law school at Notre Dame." But to name a partisan
labor leader who had energetically campaigned for Stevenson in 1952, Taft publicly declared, was "incredible."
Rank-and-file plumbers who had ignored Durkin's orders
to vote for Stevenson and supported Eisenhower resented
Taft's attitude toward the appointment. But the senator
concluded that Eisenhower had repudiated his agreement
with him on Republican policies. "I don't know whether
he realizes that," Taft said privately, "but if he doesn't he
is very stupid indeed."[3]

Eisenhower was not stupid, of course. The president-
elect expected this appointment to be "a delicate problem." He did not want a secretary of labor "who had
evinced strong views in labor-management relations . . .
particularly . . . as a supporter of socialism or as a 'union
buster.' " Yet he believed the Department of Labor should
be headed by someone with labor-management experience.
His campaign manager and attorney general-designate,
Herbert Brownell, suggested Durkin, in large part because
of the Republicans' traditional ties with the building trades
unions. Eisenhower discussed his philosophy with Durkin

before giving his stamp of approval. He told the candidate that he would be expected to represent labor in the cabinet but that his personal allegiance must henceforth belong to the nation, not to trade unionism. According to Eisenhower, Durkin "seemed to have difficulty in making this distinction . . . and also expressed concern for his future if for any reason he might find it necessary to leave the government." Eisenhower reassured him on the latter point, and a few days later Durkin notified him that the plumbers union would hold his presidency open for a year in case he wanted to return. He would become secretary of labor. Eisenhower concluded that both men thought of "the appointment as something of an experiment," but the president-elect "was committed to an attempt to minimize the mutual antagonisms which . . . were impeding progress in our economy." Durkin was the first trade unionist in twenty years to head the Department of Labor. His appointment fulfilled three unwritten rules about the composition of the cabinet: it should include a Catholic, the Department of Labor should be prolabor, and the minority party should be represented. The result, as one wit put it, was that Eisenhower's cabinet contained nine millionaires and a plumber. Although this was not literally true, Durkin felt uncomfortable around the other cabinet members and vice versa. He once confided to a friend that "every time I entered a room, they all stopped talking."[4]

Eisenhower promised in his first State of the Union message, as he had during the campaign, to take a hard look at the Taft-Hartley Act. In his message he noted that the country had five years' experience with the law, and it was clear there was a "need for corrective action, and we should promptly proceed to amend that act." *Fortune* magazine interviewed Taft before Congress assembled to hear the president's address and concluded that the Ohio senator would "be able to push through some important amendments" to his law because the "obstacles [Truman and the Democratic-controlled Eighty-second Congress?]

were pretty well removed this November." The incoming administration was committed to amending the labor policy, and the magazine concluded that "organized labor is about to acquiesce in it." *Fortune* predicted that Taft would press for changes to allow the building trades unions to operate hiring halls. He would also support permitting the building trades, maritime workers, and longshoremen to force workers to join a union shop in three to four days after being hired rather than the thirty days required in Taft-Hartley. The magazine believed he would want to extend the noncommunist affidavit to employers, to bar communists from employment after they were expelled from their union, to allow employers to avoid participation in the administration of pension funds if they wished, to let economic strikers vote in representation elections, to give the NLRB discretion in seeking injunctions against secondary boycotts, and to allow secondary boycotts on goods transferred from a struck plant to another plant. The magazine also predicted that he would favor letting the Department of Labor establish minimum standards on pension plans. All these points closely approximated Taft's current thinking.[5]

Early in his administration Eisenhower decided to appoint a committee representing labor, management, and the public to study the national labor policy. This idea was born in February 1953 after a meeting with the new Senate majority leader, Taft, and the new House Speaker, Joseph Martin, Republican from Massachusetts. Reporters caught Taft and Martin as they left the White House and quizzed them about the meeting. The congressional leaders said they had discussed a list of legislation the president wanted enacted that session and revision of Taft-Hartley was prominent on the agenda. Eisenhower "especially wanted prompt action" on labor legislation, and the issues of allowing economic strikers to vote in representation elections and requiring union officials to sign noncommunist affidavits were the two changes he particularly wanted. They reported that the president intended to appoint a select committee to study other possible amendments. The group he chose was composed of Secretary of Labor Durkin, Secretary of Commerce Sinclair Weeks, Taft, the new chairman of the Senate Committee on Labor and Public Welfare, H. Alexander Smith, a conservative Republican from New Jersey, and Representative Samuel K. McConnell, Republican from Pennsylvania and now chairman of the House Committee on Education and Labor, a man whom trade unionists regarded as moderate. Taft asked Eisenhower to appoint Bernard Shanley, a Republican politician from New Jersey and one of the president's aides, to chair the group and to serve as liaison between it and the Oval Office. In the discussions that followed, according to Shanley, he and Taft got along famously. Gerald Morgan, who had helped write the Hartley bill and the Taft-Hartley compromise bill that came out of conference in 1947, was assigned by the White House to work with Shanley on Taft-Hartley amendments.[6]

While the Shanley committee was working, the AFL and the CIO were developing their own list of changes. The AFL polled its affiliates for suggestions and named a strategy group that was dominated by the building trades. The CIO formulated its own program, and the two unions presented their views to the congressional labor committees. The CIO testified that it would support President Eisenhower's efforts to bring "fairness and justice to the law," and George Meany, president of the AFL, admitted that labor had "to stop talking about repeal and get the law changed by amendment." United Mine Workers president John L. Lewis derided both the AFL and the CIO proposals, saying it was impossible to make Taft-Hartley fair by amending it. Instead, Lewis advocated the extreme view of repealing both the Wagner and Taft-Hartley acts.[7]

Despite their differences, both major labor federations attempted to work with the Shanley committee. The AFL was represented in the administration by Durkin, and the

CIO counsel, Arthur Goldberg, was in close contact with Shanley. In addition, the administration made an abortive effort to appease the CIO by inviting it to name an assistant secretary of labor from its ranks to join the AFL representative, Durkin. The CIO subsequently named John Edelman of the textile union. The administration decided he was politically unpalatable, however, because certain members of Congress found his socialist views unacceptable. Although an investigation demonstrated his loyalty beyond doubt, the administration refused to send his nomination to the Senate. Walter Reuther wrote Sherman Adams, Eisenhower's chief of staff, who also handled patronage, that the situation resembled the harassment of Agnes Meyer and Charles "Chip" Bohlen when their nominations reached the Senate, which he labeled "character assassination." Probably the administration had the Meyer and Bohlen situations in mind when the decision was made not to forward Edelman's name to the Senate. After the bitter fight over Bohlen's nomination, Majority Leader Taft sent word back to the White House, warning "no more Bohlens." Reuther stuck to his guns and declared that the position go to Edelman or no one, and as a result the CIO was not represented in the administration. This episode increased the CIO's distrust of the Eisenhower administration.[8]

The AFL took a different approach. Two of its lawyers, J. Albert Woll and Herbert Thatcher, met with counsel representing industry and business, Gerard Reilly and Theodore Iserman (who had helped write the Taft-Hartley Act), and John C. Gall and Burton Zorn, to discuss "unofficially" some possible compromises. By 20 June they had reached agreement on several changes, including prehire agreements in the building trades, extending voting rights to economic strikers, eliminating the noncommunist affidavit, and limiting mandatory injunctions. In late June they discussed remaining differences with Bernard Shanley and Gerald Morgan. These discussions proved to be inconclusive, however, because Shanley was discovering that the Departments of Commerce and Labor, and particularly their secretaries, Weeks and Durkin, were far apart in their views and these differences were reflected in this unofficial group.[9]

Secretary of Commerce Weeks was a Boston manufacturer of metal products, whose father also had been a businessman and secretary of war under Presidents Warren Harding and Calvin Coolidge. Weeks was well known as a fund-raiser and, because he was an early supporter of Eisenhower, was named to head the finance committee for the campaign of 1952. Unlike Taft, who did not think good businessmen automatically made good government administrators, Weeks applauded Eisenhower's appointment of businessmen to the cabinet instead of giving "high priority to the theories of Socialists or to the notions of local egg-heads." *U.S. News & World Report* lauded Weeks for sacrificing a six-figure salary to run the Department of Commerce for $22,000 a year. Weeks took a hard-headed businessman's approach to labor policy, and most of his views eventually prevailed, both in his department and in the cabinet.[10]

In late May Shanley began meeting separately with spokesmen from the Commerce and Labor departments to discuss the two proposals. Durkin, Shanley soon discovered, "would not take off his AFL hat and made no serious decision without discussing it with George Meany." Shanley was so certain of this collusion that he had Durkin followed several times after committee meetings and told Taft that Durkin invariably "would walk across the park to the A.F. of L. building and consult with Meany and whatever we agreed to went right out of the window." So Shanley was not surprised when Weeks found that Durkin's proposals "were strictly the union mind and the same thing that [Maurice] Tobin, the former Secretary of Labor, would have produced had he been in command."[11]

Eisenhower's aide also had his troubles with Weeks. He

was particularly irritated when Weeks, making no progress with Shanley, went over his head, writing a memorandum to Eisenhower explaining the Commerce Department's difficulties with Durkin. Shanley told the president that the Weeks memorandum was "reactionary" and that Labor and Commerce were "180 degrees apart." A short time later Shanley and Morgan met with Steve Dunn, counsel for the Department of Commerce, to discuss the impasse. Morgan was a good friend of Dunn "and just gave him plain hell about the position they [Commerce] were taking which was completely reactionary as he pointed out and inconsistent to boot." This explosion had its desired effect as "Dunn completely colapsed [sic] and exceeded [acceded] to all the ordinary amendments, which we had agreed to with the Secretary of Labor and his group." When the full committee met in Taft's office on 23 June, Shanley reported the senator as "almost aesthetic [ecstatic]" over the progress made. The presidential aide was overly optimistic about Taft's support at this point because the senator would never acquiesce to some of Durkin's prounion points, especially repeal of Section 14(b) and approval of certain types of secondary boycotts. On 16 July Shanley and Morgan "did the finishing touches on our masterpiece—the Taft-Hartley Act." By that time, the AFL had repudiated the agreement its lawyers had reached with the lawyers of industry. This rejection by the AFL executive council disturbed Shanley only because its support for changing the secondary boycott " would have been a great help in putting the whole picture together."[12]

Shanley put the final proposal together and wrote a message for Eisenhower to send with it to Congress. After Commerce and Labor received their copies, Shanley and Sherman Adams met with Steve Dunn. "It was not a pleasant session." Dunn's response to the proposed amendments was "who won the election?" and he remarked that "industry is back where it was in the early part of the century." Adams responded that "Commerce is living in the dark ages." Weeks, Shanley reported, was "very shy obviously" about the draft that he had received. Durkin, however, was "quite elated about it."[13]

The proposal contained nineteen changes in the national labor policy, many of which were promoted by unions supporting the Republican party. First, it would exempt small employers from the law and provide for the secretaries of labor and commerce and the chairmen of the Senate and House labor committees to review administration of the law and make recommendations accordingly. It would satisfy the request of some of the AFL affiliates by narrowing the definition of the term *supervisor* and would permit a union to discharge an employee who lost his membership because he had disclosed confidential union information or was found to be in sympathy with the Communist party or other subversive organizations. It would also limit the union's responsibility for actions of its members when that responsibility arose solely by reason of their membership in the union and would authorize union-employer agreements for minimum training or experience for employment. In a closely related AFL demand, it would authorize the construction, amusement, maritime, and longshoremen's unions to require union membership within seven days after employment. It would abolish employees' rights to require their union to negotiate a union-shop agreement. It proposed relaxing rules on certain types of secondary boycotts and removing the requirement that the NLRB general counsel seek injunctions against all secondary boycotts and, instead, give him discretionary powers over them. The Taft-Hartley "cooling off" period between issuing the injunction and the report of the board of inquiry would be reduced from sixty to thirty days. The proposed amendment would prohibit a representational election for four months after the beginning of a strike, even when strikers had been replaced by other workers. Parties to a collective bargaining agreement would be relieved from obligation to bargain on subjects not covered by the agreement until the termination of the agreement. The proposal would limit the types of information unions had to file with the secretary of labor and eliminate both the noncommunist affidavit and Section 14(b) that permited state right-to-work laws. Finally, it would allow the checkoff authorization until revoked by the employee and permit employers to waive the right to participate in the administration of union welfare funds if they desired.

It was no wonder that Durkin was elated with the proposals and that management, when apprised of them, was outraged. The legal department of the Youngstown Sheet and Tube Company believed that these proposals were made because certain labor leaders promised that, if they were enacted, they would support the Republicans in the elections of 1954.[14] Fourteen of the nineteen proposals, however, had been supported in Congress in 1949 by John S. Wood, Democrat from Georgia, when he attempted to outflank the Truman administration's efforts to get the Taft-Hartley Act repealed. In addition, Senators Smith and Taft had proposed several of the same changes in previous attempts to amend the Taft-Hartley Act after 1949. Copies of the proposed amendments were sent to the secretaries of labor and commerce and to Senator Smith and Representative McConnell.

Robert Taft died the day that Eisenhower was to send the proposed amendments to Congress. Taft had been in considerable pain for the previous four months, and on 31 August 1953 he succumbed to cancer and a brain hemorrhage. His death brought an end to Eisenhower's accommodationist policy. Only a Republican with Taft's prestige could have pressed the nineteen amendments through Congress (and even he would not have supported some of the proposals), and in his absence no one would be able to push through the changes he supported. The election of William Knowland of California as the new Senate majority leader signaled the beginning of Eisenhower's woes with the right wing of his party, which would plague the last six years of his administration, when conservatives dominated the Republican leadership in Congress.

Sinclair Weeks initiated an assault against Durkin's nineteen proposals even before they were made public. He asked prestigious industrial leaders to mount a campaign of protest through letters, telephone calls, and personal contacts directed at Smith, McConnell, and Vice-President Richard Nixon. In addition, Senator Smith forwarded to Bernard Shanley a sharp critique of the amendments that had been drafted by Thomas Shroyer, one of the counsel who had worked closely with Taft on the Taft-Hartley Act. Smith concluded that it would be impolitic for Eisenhower to send to Congress the message and the proposed amendments, some of which Taft had opposed, on the day of the senator's death. Smith also concurred with Shroyer's opposition to approving certain types of secondary boycotts, to the expulsion of union members for disclosing union information, to barring a representational election during a strike, and to repeal of Section 14(b). Sherman Adams agreed that the timing was inappropriate, and the message was not sent. Taft's death ended organized labor's last best hope for amending Taft-Hartley to its satisfaction.[15]

Durkin granted an interview to Ed Lahey, and the gist of the nineteen points soon appeared in the *Chicago Daily News*. Shortly thereafter, Steve Dunn released the proposed message and amendments to the National Association of Manufacturers and the press. The *Wall Street Journal* published the entire program verbatim on 3 August 1953. Four days later, when Shanley met with Weeks, the aide had done an about-face. Shanley apparently decided that Weeks had demonstrated real political clout. The presidential aide had previously observed in his diary that Weeks was living in the dark ages in opposing the Durkin program but now abjectly surrendered by assuring the secretary of commerce that the program would never have gone to Congress without his approval. The *Wall Street Journal* story had enraged the nation's business leaders and the right wing of the Republican party, and the White House soon received the full force of their wrath. *Newsweek* reported that "so voluminous and acrimonious was the mail that Presidential aides began answering it with a form letter that minimized the message as a 'working draft.' " On 10 August Shanley, Sherman Adams, Gerald Morgan, and Wilton "Jerry" Persons, Eisenhower's congressional liaison, met to discuss the situation. They agreed that, with Congress adjourned, the message would have to wait indefinitely but that the president should send a message to the upcoming AFL annual convention about the administration's work on Taft-Hartley amendments. When Shanley reported all these developments to Eisenhower, the president promised him that "if you have proof as to who did it [leaked the proposals to the press], I'll fire him." Apparently Shanley was afraid to tell Eisenhower that the leak had come from Weeks or his immediate subordinate Dunn. Shanley now called it the "working draft of the Taft-Hartley message" and described Eisenhower as "literally wild." "We are not living in the dark ages," the President raged, "and Weeks would have to recognize it and that Durkin would have to be reasonable as well." Shanley suggested that Eisenhower talk to Durkin when he went to New York City to deliver a speech. The two also discussed appointing a new secretary of labor. Eisenhower asked Shanley to take the job, but he declined and, instead, "highly recommended" James P. Mitchell, who had been suggested by his friend William Brennan, a later Eisenhower appointee to the Supreme Court. Shanley also became convinced that the National Association of Manufacturers and the United States Chamber of Commerce had begun "an insidious campaign" to get him out of the White House, which was probably true.[16]

Eisenhower met Durkin in New York City on 19 August. According to Eisenhower, Durkin informed him that unless the president followed through with the proposed nineteen changes, his union would disown him and he would be out of a job when his government service ended. Eisenhower asked him to continue to work with the staff on the proposed amendments and thought Durkin promised to do so. But two weeks later the secretary of labor sent in his resignation, which Eisenhower accepted. The two men had a further discussion on 10 September at which Eisenhower said Durkin complained that Shanley and Morgan had broken faith with him and that he understood that Eisenhower had agreed to support the nineteen amendments. Eisenhower informed him that they were still "under consideration."[17]

Durkin's version of these discussions differed considerably from the president's. According to Durkin, Shanley and Morgan informed the president of developments in the committee meetings, he approved the nineteen amendments, and he would not allow the secretary of commerce to veto any of them. At the 19 August meeting the president and the secretary of labor discussed the leak to the press and agreed that it "in no way lessened the need" to release the agreed-to nineteen points, even though Congress was no longer in session. When the White House staff proved adamant about reopening discussions on the proposals over the next two weeks, Durkin submitted his resignation in protest. According to Durkin, on 10 September Eisenhower informed him that he had changed his mind and could no longer accept the nineteen amendments.[18]

There is no doubt that Durkin was correct in feeling betrayed, but it was Bernard Shanley who misled him. When Shanley reported that Durkin was elated with the proposed amendments on 31 July, the secretary of labor obviously was convinced that Shanley and Morgan had sold Eisenhower irrevocably on the proposals and that he had won an important victory for unions. Significantly, the version printed in the *Wall Street Journal* bore the label "The White House," which could lead Durkin to believe, especially when he wanted to, that Eisenhower had initially approved the nineteen points but changed his mind under pressure from business interests. Others involved in the negotiations believed the president could not be put in a position that would not allow him to change his mind and that no binding agreement had been reached, or at least not one as absolute as Durkin was convinced he had obtained. Representative McConnell still considered the proposal a "working draft." Senators Smith and Leverett Saltonstall, Republican from Massachusetts, substantiated Eisenhower's disclaimer that he had made definite promises to Durkin.[19] Sinclair Weeks had won the first round in the effort to modify Taft-Hartley, and Eisenhower began to abandon his attempts to woo labor leaders through legislative reform to support the Republican party.

Eisenhower chose James P. Mitchell to replace Durkin. Mitchell was a vice-president of Bloomingdale Brothers department stores in charge of labor relations and had been recommended to the president by Shanley and Secretary of Defense Charles Wilson. When asked his opinion of Mitchell, George Meany replied that "he is a very fine gentleman, a very fine fellow and I think he will be as good a Secretary of Labor as Brother Weeks allows him to be. There are definite indications that Weeks considers himself part of the Labor Department, at least as an overseer." But Eisenhower found that Mitchell agreed with "the need for economic statesmanship on both sides of the bargaining table" to bring labor into the corporate commonwealth. His ability to win the support of union members, as opposed to leaders and management led the president to conclude that "there would be no need to appoint a successor to him."[20]

Mitchell had received considerable experience in labor relations as a protégé of Brehon Somervell. When Somervell headed the New York City branch of the Works Progress Administration, Mitchell had handled labor relations for him. Left-wing groups in New York City had appealed to the unemployed during the Great Depression, and Mitchell's recollection of that phase of his career was "of always having to cross a picket line to go to work in the morning." During World War II Somervell headed the Supply Service for the Department of War, and he put Mitchell in charge of personnel. Following the war Mitchell headed personnel and labor relations at Macy's and then at Bloomingdale's. Before becoming secretary of labor, he had served four months as an assistant secretary of the army and had won the approval of Charles Wilson. He was described as having "bristling hair" and "huge shoulders" and as a personnel executive who "feels that trade unions are here to stay and that business should . . . view them as a challenge." The Senate confirmed Mitchell's appointment unanimously the day after it received the nomination, and he was sworn in on 9 October.[21]

Two months later the new secretary of labor told the annual CIO convention to be "realistic" and stop talking about repeal of the Taft-Hartley Act, but the delegates endorsed a resolution accusing Eisenhower of failing to keep his campaign pledge to make the law "fair." Eisenhower sent a message to the annual AFL convention that year, read by Vice-President Nixon, in which he called attention to Shanley's committee, which was still working on Taft-Hartley amendments. "The wealth of knowledge and experience . . . of Durkin . . . was an asset of great value," he declared, and "losing the benefit of that knowledge and experience was considered unfortunate by me and by every member of the committee." But he promised the delegates that the Shanley committee would continue its quest and would make recommendations to him "before the end of the year." In December the president was asked his opinion of right-to-work laws. He carefully avoided committing himself by responding that Congress should seriously consider amending Taft-Hartley. Until "this thing is exhaustively and completely argued out, I just don't know what my decision will be."[22]

On 21 November Mitchell felt ready to begin work on Taft-Hartley. He met with White House aides Shanley,

Morgan, Max Raab, and Jack Martin to discuss the nine-teen amendments. They "cut out a few items which seemed unnecessary" and, at Mitchell's suggestion, added a provision allowing workers to take a secret ballot before striking. This "would have tremendous appeal to Sinny Weeks with the consequent result that we felt quite certain that he would back the whole program," Shanley recorded. Mitchell wanted to abolish Section 14(b) but was warned that such a move would lose support among southerners "and the support of McConnell and without him it of course would be impossible to put the program through the House." During the next several years Mitchell successfully fought efforts by Senator Barry Goldwater, Republican of Arizona, to secure passage of a national right-to-work law. "It was a plan," Shanley assured the group, "which Senator Taft would have fully approved" and it "was important to say that to the leadership." After Mitchell left, Shanley asked Morgan and Martin their opinion of the new secretary of labor. "With glowing eyes," they described him as "a terrific fellow . . . and his whole attitude was so much quicker than Durkin's."[23]

Mitchell presented the revised proposals at a cabinet meeting on 15 December. Henry Cabot Lodge recommended that Eisenhower speak in generalizations regarding Taft-Hartley in his upcoming State of the Union message. "Labor leaders are stuck with calling Taft-Hartley slave labor," he argued. "Congress is not unhappy with it. So let labor leaders worry, not get us stuck [with specifics]." The president responded that it was "a congressional matter, where I have to give some lead—but accept what Congress does, within certain limits." Mitchell observed that he would agree with Lodge, except for Eisenhower's promises on Taft-Hartley, and "we have to follow through" with recommendations. Weeks noted that he and Mitchell had worked hard to reach an agreement on the proposed amendments. "We each have some mental reservations," he admitted, "but we agreed." Nixon observed that Mitchell's proposals were good ones. "Regardless of what we do, [we] won't get labor leaders for us," and, he noted, it would set "the tone to this whole administration in regard to it being liberal, middle-of-the-road, or conservative. People will see we are liberalizing Taft-Hartley," he added.[24]

As a result of this exchange, Eisenhower was vague on labor legislation in his State of the Union message, but he promised to speak to Congress on the topic in the immediate future. On 11 January 1954, he submitted his recommendations for amending the Taft-Hartley Act. The number of proposals was now reduced to fourteen. He wanted to amend the law so that when a Taft-Hartley injunction was issued, a special local board would meet immediately with both parties to seek a settlement of the dispute. In secondary boycott cases, seeking an injunction would be discretionary. He thought the law should be clarified to permit secondary boycotts when an employer was performing "farmed-out" work for another employer whose workers were striking and when the struck employer was working on a construction site with other employers. Economic strikers should be permitted to vote in representation elections, and for four months after a strike the NLRB could not consider a petition from another union claiming to represent the strikers. He proposed that neither party to a collective bargaining agreement should be required to negotiate on issues outside the agreement during its term, unless the contract permitted it or by mutual agreement. He recommended that during a national emergency strike, the president be allowed to reconvene the board of inquiry after it made its report in the required sixty days and ask for its recommendations for ending the strike. The construction, amusement, and maritime industries would be permitted to establish prehiring agreements, which they were already doing sub rosa, and to require union membership within seven days of employment. A union should not be held legally responsible for the actions of its members, and the noncommunist affidavit should be extended to employers. Free speech should apply equally to labor and management in every aspect of their relationship. He recommended that Congress make a thorough investigation of union welfare and pension funds and clarify the law to make certain that states would have the power to protect the health and safety of their citizens during labor disputes; he wanted workers to vote on calling a strike by secret ballot "held under Government auspices" and for the checkoff to continue through the life of a contract unless the worker revoked its authorization. The proposals to which Taft had objected—the redefinition of supervisors, the elimination of the union-shop deauthorization election, allowing hiring halls to determine work qualifications, permitting unions to fire a worker for disclosure of confidential union information, and eliminating Section 14(b)—were not included in these recommendations. Shanley informed Eisenhower that Taft had "felt that the section [14(b)] was wrong in principle, but he was opposed to repealing it." Taft would have supported Eisenhower's fourteen amendments of 1954 even though some of his supporters would have been disappointed in him for doing so.[25]

Eisenhower's recommendation on strike votes caused an immediate uproar. Senator H. Alexander Smith had introduced legislation calling for a poststrike vote. It was unclear whether Eisenhower was recommending a prestrike or poststrike vote. When queried, Shanley and Morgan said the White House approved Smith's version. When Weeks heard this, he was shocked because he had insisted during the negotiations that the vote must precede a strike.[26]

Eisenhower held a press conference two days after he sent his labor message to Congress, and the first question reporters asked him concerned the strike vote. Eisenhower was the first president to allow press conferences to be televised, and he soon became adept at garbling his syntax and confusing reporters by obscuring the issues. When James Hagerty, his press secretary, once expressed concern

over a question reporters might ask in an impending press
conference, Eisenhower reassured him, "Don't worry, Jim,
if that question comes up, I'll just confuse them." His response in this instance is worth quoting in full:

Actually, of course, what I was trying to establish was a principle.
Nearly all the suggestions I made for the amendment of the Taft-
Hartley Act were in that tenor, that here is something that should be
done. I have carefully avoided the exact details of how these things
should be done, because we well know that is a province of the Congress and its committees in their investigations.
   My function, as I see it, is to lay down for their consideration the
things that I believe to be principle, and that is exactly what I tried
to do there.
   So I would accept anything that looks the most practicable and
feasible in the circumstances.

This is an example of Eisenhower's obfuscation at its
best.[27]
   Arthur Goldberg decided to publicize Eisenhower's
strike proposal. He got statements from William Davis,
former chairman of the National War Labor Board (NWLB),
Jesse Freidan, former general counsel for the NWLB, and
Theodore Kheel, former executive director of the NWLB,
declaring that during World War II the board had not found
strike polls of workers to be "a useful expedient for mini-
mizing strikes." He then published their statements as advertisements in the *New York Times*, the *New York Post*,
the *Washington Post*, the *Washington Star*, and the *Wall
Street Journal*.[28]
   Most leaders of organized labor opposed Eisenhower's
changes. Speaking for the CIO, Walter Reuther said the
proposals "would make Taft-Hartley even worse than it is. . . .
This bill would not rid Taft-Hartley of its union-busting
provisions as the President pledged during the campaign.
Rather it adds new ones." The AFL, however, representing
the conflicting interests of its constituents, admitted that
the proposal contained some meritorious points, but over-

all it was "woefully short of the corrections needed."[29]
Some AFL affiliates supported some of the changes.

Two months later, after brief hearings, Smith's committee, by a party vote of seven to six, recommended the
amendments to the Senate. The majority made two prolabor changes in Eisenhower's proposals: the strike vote requirement was eliminated and the free speech provision
was rewritten so as to benefit unions more than management. Union officials worried that the more conservative
House committee was rewriting Eisenhower's recommendations to place more curbs on unions. Union strategy thus
was to get the Senate bill recommitted and hold the House
proposal in committee.

Debate began in the Senate on 3 May. Senator Smith introduced the committee bill by noting that the president's
proposals were consistent with Eisenhower's middle-of-
the-road philosophy on important social and economic
policies. The Republican majority on the committee had
voted, over the objection of the minority Democrats, to
support Smith's opening announcement that the committee's investigations and recommendations would be limited to Eisenhower's fourteen proposals. In 1953, Smith
reported, the House and Senate labor committees had held
extensive hearings on all aspects of labor policy that resulted in sixteen volumes of testimony. "The subject has
been thoroughly studied up and down and across the
board," he explained in justifying his committee's limited
approach. By confining its inquiry to the fourteen proposals, the committee was able to report quickly to the Senate. Senators Paul Douglas, Democrat from Illinois, and
John F. Kennedy, Democrat from Massachusetts, were permitted to propose a series of amendments to Eisenhower's
recommendations in executive session, but they were defeated by a strict party vote of seven to six. The minority
was not permitted to propose amendments in a minority
report.[30]

That same day Barry Goldwater, Republican from Arizona, introduced a proposal to tighten the language of the amendment that would allow states to protect the health and safety of citizens during labor disputes. He insisted that he had received approval from the proper White House aides. Senator Smith supported his claim, although he was not certain that the president had seen the exact language of the Goldwater amendment. Senator William Purtell, Republican from Connecticut, offered an amendment restoring the secret prestrike vote for workers. On 7 May Senator Lister Hill, Democrat from Alabama, moved to recommit the bill to the committee. The vote was fifty yes, forty-two no, along party lines. Senate Minority Leader Lyndon B. Johnson, Democrat from Texas, worked hard to consolidate his party on the issue. He stressed the need for party unity in the upcoming elections and promised some senators labor support for a 90 percent parity farm bill. In addition, some southern senators opposed Eisenhower's proposals as being too prolabor. As a result, every Democrat voted to recommit, along with Independent Wayne Morse from Oregon and three Republicans, maverick William Langer of North Dakota and conservatives Milton Young of North Dakota and George Malone of Nevada. When meeting with legislative leaders, Eisenhower angrily observed that these three were "not Republicans anyway." Many Republicans were glad not to have to take a position on some of the changes. After the vote was taken, Smith was reported to be "cheerful as a dicky bird."[31]

The administration did not again seriously consider revision of Taft-Hartley until 1958. In a message to the AFL convention in 1954, Eisenhower expressed "regret over the failure to amend Taft-Hartley," but pointed out that the Democrats had defeated his proposals. He promised to recommend again the "economic strikers" provision and the elimination of the noncommunist affidavit because "it is completely un-American." In his State of the Union message in 1955, he renewed his call for the fourteen amendments, especially for economic strikers and the noncommunist affidavit. In his message in 1956 he merely said the fourteen amendments "should be enacted without further delay."

Benjamin Aaron concluded that the urgency for amending Taft-Hartley waned during the 1950s because it did not become the slave labor law union leaders had predicted. Continued prosperity calmed fears that the law would adversely affect wages, hours, and working conditions, and labor-management relations steadily improved in most parts of the nation, even in the South. Thus, Aaron noted, the law did not present "a substantial and serious threat to the institution of unionism and to the welfare of workers."[32]

In addition, during the mid-1950s union leaders were busy with other concerns. In 1955 they succeeded in obtaining an increase in the minimum wage, which the administration wanted to raise from $.75 to $.90 and Senator Paul Douglas wanted raised to $1.10. Congress compromised on $1.00. In the same year the United Auto Workers won a guaranteed annual wage (GAW), and the AFL and CIO merged to form the AFL-CIO.

Walter Reuther pressed for a GAW in the automobile industry to offset the seasonal nature of the work. General Motors soon followed Ford Motor Company in agreeing to contribute an amount for each hour worked to a special fund. Money would be paid from this fund to supplement state unemployment benefits to equal a certain percentage of the worker's normal earnings. One Ford official claimed this "was neither guaranteed nor annual nor a wage" because in a depression the small fund would be quickly depleted. But the UAW regarded the GAW as a major milestone toward economic security.[33]

Labor unity was finally achieved in 1955. When the long-time rivals William Green and Phillip Murray died within a month of each other in 1952, the AFL chose George Meany of the plumbers union as president and the CIO elected Walter Reuther. Both men pushed for unification of the two unions. Meany said that when he was elected president, the only instruction the executive council gave him was "to try and end the rift in the American labor movement." The next year these unions took a major step toward that goal when they signed a nonraiding pact that allowed peaceful negotiations to proceed between the two giants of labor. Two years of discussions led to the signing of a merger pact in 1955 and the election of George Meany as president of some 15 million workers. This unification was made possible by the CIO's expelling its communist members who opposed the merger, by the emergence of younger leaders who did not feel the bitterness of the great split during the 1930s, and by the belief that the national government was controlled by business interests hostile to the programs and policies organized labor had supported for two decades.[34] Of course, the merger did not end old feuds and differences of opinion and philosophy. For years the various affiliates remained at odds with each other on labor policy issues and had conflicting goals, desires, and even jurisdictions.

Organized labor had good reason to worry about the business orientation of the Eisenhower administration. The new administration soon changed the composition of the NLRB, with long-term and far-reaching consequences. In early 1953 the president appointed Guy Farmer, a Washington management lawyer, and Philip Ray Rodgers, clerk of the Senate Labor Committee and former Taft aide, to the NLRB. When he appointed Albert C. Beeson, an industrial relations manager from a California firm, to the board in 1955, the NLRB had a Republican majority for the first time in its history. Almost immediately the board began to reverse NLRB precedents, in most cases favoring management.[35]

In seeking advice for these appointments, Eisenhower found his aides sharply divided. In 1953 Gerard Reilly and Theodore Iserman circulated a memorandum that was supported by Gerald Morgan. They recommended that the current prolabor NLRB be brought in line with administration policy by nominating the "right people" for board membership and soon won the support of large national firms that were members of the National Association of Manufacturers and the U.S. Chamber of Commerce. This became the official policy of the NAM. Small business members of those management organizations, however, argued that Eisenhower's appointments would not affect the NLRB's regional personnel, whom they wished replaced, and they sought instead an end to federal preemption on subjects covered by Taft-Hartley. They wanted to abolish the NLRB and have district courts adjudicate labor-management issues.

Administration advisers were similarly divided. The Department of Labor, under Martin Durkin, wanted no changes in the NLRB, which reflected the desires of the AFL and CIO. The Department of Commerce, under Sinclair Weeks, initially supported the small manufacturers, but pressure from large national employers eventually forced the department to shift and endorse the NAM position. Because he received such conflicting advice, Eisenhower made no recommendations to Congress in 1953 or 1954 to change the NLRB and instead brought major changes in NLRB policy through his appointments.

The congressional labor committees were similarly divided. The House committee held a series of hearings in 1953 for the purpose of abolishing the NLRB, but the committee was evenly divided between liberals and the conservative coalition and could not agree on a recommendation. When the Reilly-Iserman-Morgan policy won out in the administration, the conservative House Labor Committee chairman, Sam McConnell, felt betrayed. But Morgan assured him that Eisenhower would give him "a good board."

The Senate committee on Labor and Public Welfare had the dual function of preparing labor legislation and making recommendations to the Senate on NLRB nominations. No strong opposition to the Farmer and Rodgers appointments surfaced in the Senate committee. But when Beeson's name came before the senators, liberals concluded that he would represent a swing vote because the NLRB was then composed of two Truman appointees and two Eisenhower men. Led by John Kennedy, the Senate Labor Committee conducted an extensive three-week review of Beeson's background, and he was confirmed for an unexpired ten-month term by the close vote of forty-five to forty-two, the Senate dividing along party lines. When his term expired, the Department of Labor supported Dwight Shugrue, one of Senator Irving Ives's administrative assistants, and the Department of Commerce wanted Michael Bernstein, counsel to the Republicans on the Senate Labor Commit-tee. Commerce and Labor finally compromised on Boyd Leedom, a member of the South Dakota Supreme Court. South Dakota Senator Karl Mundt defended his nomina-tion on the grounds that his state had no large industries or labor organizations and, therefore, no "controversial prob-lems" in labor-management relations, and Leedom was easily confirmed. Thus the Eisenhower Republicans had a majority on the NLRB, and by the end of 1954 the NAM happily reported that the new board had "overturned long-established rulings, and have given the Act a new, and al-most always anti-labor meaning. . . . They have proceeded to imbue the Board with the employer-oriented interests of the new Administration."[36]

In 1955, the secretary of labor reviewed one of Eisen-hower's 1954 recommendations and suggested that Con-gress require unions to report on welfare and pension funds, an issue that was growing in importance. He also discussed with Republican legislative leaders the need for women to receive equal pay for equal work. Under Mitch-ell's guidance, following the defeat in 1954 of the Taft-Hart-ley amendments, the Eisenhower administration began to stress the economic well-being of laborers and press for fur-ther economic gains while ignoring possible changes in labor policy. Mitchell had signaled the new approach in his first message to the annual CIO convention in 1953. In that speech he devoted as much time to the need for raising the minimum wage and extending its coverage as he did to the Taft-Hartley amendments then being considered.

In his State of the Union message in 1957, the president did not mention amending the Taft-Hartley Act. This new labor strategy appeared to be working politically. In 1952 millions of Americans who traditionally supported Democrats had voted for Eisenhower. Four years later the Republicans campaigned on the positive issues of peace, prosperity, and domestic unity. In the election of 1956, Eisenhower received a plurality of 9 million votes, or 3 million more than in 1952, and millions of these votes again came from laborers who had voted the Democratic ticket during the New Deal and Fair Deal years. They were enjoying Eisenhower prosperity. Years later even George Meany admitted that in the 1950s unions made great progress in health, education, and medical care, and he attributed these gains to Undersecretary Nelson Rockefeller, who was running the Department of Health, Education and Welfare (HEW), rather than to Secretary of HEW Oveta Culp Hobby.[37]

By 1957 the nation's attention was riveted on a quite different labor union issue. By that time the McClellan Committee was inflaming public and congressional opinion with revelations of widespread corruption and racketeering in the teamsters and several other national unions.

3. Enter Mr. Beck
. . . and Mr. Hoffa

While the Eisenhower administration was developing proposed amendments to Taft-Hartley, former congressman Fred Hartley sent a statement of his views on the labor-management scene to each member of Congress. Hartley was particularly incensed that "the present palace guard" was ignoring the need to protect the rights of individual workers. Hartley pointed out that his original bill had contained a "bill of rights" for the American worker but that he was forced to remove it in the conference committee. Congress should reexamine his proposal, he asserted, in rewriting the Taft-Hartley Act. These rights included secret ballots for calling a strike, for deciding union fiscal policies, and for electing union officers, and the right of the worker and his family to be free of threats of violence because of his actions or beliefs. By 1953 this concern over violence and intimidation in the labor movement was mounting as it was discovered that gangsters and racketeers had indeed infiltrated several unions.[1]

From 1950 to 1951, Senator Estes Kefauver, Tennessee Democrat, held a series of spectacular and unprecedented hearings on organized crime in large American cities. The Kefauver Committee hearings on the West Coast and in New York City were carried on the relatively new medium of television. The results were phenomenal: millions of schoolchildren and adults interrupted their daily routine to view the hearings that established television as a medium to be reckoned with in politics. In New York City the committee interrogated Frank Costello, Joe Adonis, and other underworld characters and discovered, along with other criminal revelations, shocking corruption in the International Longshoremen's Association (ILA).[2]

The Kefauver Committee discovery caught the attention of George Meany, the new president of the AFL. Meany, as Robert Kennedy noted, was gruff and stubborn, but he was also incorruptible and determined to rid his AFL of wrongdoing. As Kennedy observed, "the labor movement was fortunate to have him in an hour of crisis." Meany had heard reports as early as 1952 about misdeeds in the garment industry. Union president David Dubinsky complained that racketeers were being issued local union charters by a few AFL unions in New York City. Meany took immediate action to expel those "paper locals."[3]

When Meany read the Kefauver reports on the New York City longshoremen, he immediately attacked the problem. He persuaded the AFL executive council to expel the union for corrupt activities. Protection of the autonomous rights of individual affiliates had always been of concern to the AFL, but Meany persuaded the executive council to stipulate that a union could not use this principle to cloak illegal activity and still remain in the AFL. The AFL national convention in 1953 endorsed this new interpretation by a vote of over 72,000 to 750, and the ILA subsequently was expelled. The AFL then launched a rival union, the International Brotherhood of Longshoremen, to capture ILA membership. The new union grew slowly, however, because of the atmosphere of intimidation among the workers. As George Meany noted, his "biggest stumbling block is fear, absolute and complete fear on the part of these workers—fear for their lives, fear for their well-being, fear for their economic future." The longshoremen were in the grip of gangsters, he added, and if they could have a secret ballot, they would choose "a decent union."[4]

Long before the Kefauver Committee hearings, some

congressmen were convinced that racketeering was widespread in unions and should be investigated and exposed.
Clare E. Hoffman, Republican from Michigan, had been so
enraged by the sit-down strikes of the UAW in the 1930s
that he was relentlessly antiunion for the rest of his life.
During the June 1937 strike at Republic Steel in Monroe,
Michigan, Congressman Hoffman wired the mayor that he
would be willing to bring a "group of peaceably inclined
but armed and well-equipped citizens to aid in the defense
of your city." During the next ten years, he sponsored 34 of
the 161 major labor bills introduced in Congress to curb
the power of unions and thus established a reputation for
being rabidly antiunion. By 1959 he had introduced 135 labor bills and resolutions in the House of Representatives.[5]
   In June 1953 Hoffman became the driving force behind
efforts of the House Education and Labor Subcommittee to
investigate corruption in the jukebox and vending machine
businesses in Detroit and its ties to the international
teamsters union (the complete name is International
Brotherhoood of Teamsters, Chauffeurs, Warehousemen,
and Helpers of America). Wint Smith, Republican from
Kansas, was the chairman of the subcommittee. Smith and
Hoffman took testimony concerning terrorist tactics such
as bombings used in teamster organizational drives. James
R. (Jimmy) Hoffa, president of the Central States Teamsters Conference and an international vice-president,
quickly obtained Payne Ratner of Wichita, Kansas, as legal
counsel. Ratner had been governor of Kansas when Smith
headed the Kansas Highway Patrol. Ratner visited his old
friend Smith, and the investigation soon terminated. Smith
told reporters that orders to halt the hearings came from
"high up" and refused to elaborate on this statement.
When the McClellan Committee quizzed Ratner several
years later, he responded that he did not ask that the hearings be called off but that "they be postponed because a
state grand jury was investigating Mr. Hoffa at the time."[6]
   The following year the House Government Operations

Committee voted nineteen to one, with Hoffman dissenting, against Hoffman's proposal to look into the teamsters
union. The committee voted instead to name George
Bender, an Ohio Republican, to chair a subcommittee to
investigate Eugene (Jimmy) James, secretary-treasurer of
the International Laundry Workers Union. They wanted to
know about his ties to the teamsters and, specifically,
about a check for $5,625 from his union to Sid Brennan,
head of the Minneapolis teamsters, to help repay a "loan"
from his union's welfare fund. But key witnesses pleaded
the Fifth Amendment and the hearings had little impact. A
turning point came when the chairman of the House Labor
Committee, Sam McConnell, hired Carmine Bellino, a top-
notch accountant formerly with the FBI. Bellino, together
with the committee's chief counsel, Edward McCabe, examined the sheet metal workers union and found payoffs
and bribery in obtaining union insurance and a murder
that was connected with control over the union's health
and welfare funds in its western area. They also uncovered
bits of evidence of scandal in Dave Beck's Western Conference of Teamsters. But McConnell decided only that
"there were some unanswered questions" he hoped to get
answered later, and the investigation was dropped. None of
these probes had any national impact until the teamsters
international was examined.[7]

The teamsters began in 1903 as an organization representing workers driving delivery wagons in the large cities.
From 1907 to 1952 they were led by Daniel Tobin, a powerful unionist who became a confidant of presidents of the
United States. During Tobin's presidency in the first half
of the twentieth century, the teamsters organized all types
of truck drivers, including over-the-road drivers in inter-
state commerce. But Tobin was a craft unionist of the
Gompers-Green mold and opposed the mass unionism of
the CIO. Younger leaders such as Dave Beck disagreed
with what they considered an old-fashioned way of
thinking.

Beck, a vain and pompous man, was a poor boy who began as a laundry wagon driver in Seattle and worked up to be president of the Western Conference of Teamsters. In 1952 he succeeded Tobin as the international president. By the mid-1950s the teamsters had grown to over 1.5 million members, which made it the nation's largest union, and had accumulated huge welfare and pension funds. Dave Beck, in charge of those funds, was callously misusing them for his personal benefit, but, with the failure of the Smith and Bender investigation, he had little fear of exposure. Then in 1956, when investigations were renewed, with the help of a determinedly aggressive new chief counsel, the probing of corrupt union activities took a new turn.

After Adlai Stevenson received the Democratic presidential nomination in 1956, he made the startling decision to throw the vice-presidential nomination open to the convention. In the ensuing melee, Senator Estes Kefauver of Tennessee was challenged by John F. Kennedy, a senator from Massachusetts, who had defeated Henry Cabot Lodge in the Eisenhower landslide of 1952. In the ensuing four years, the youthful senator had sponsored no major legislation and was regarded by his colleagues and by reporters as a wealthy playboy. John and his younger brother Robert came from a family that was knowledgeable in politics, and considering their lack of time to organize at the convention, they performed well even though Kennedy lost the nomination to Kefauver. This episode apparently made a significant impact on John Kennedy in at least two ways. First, he determined to seek the Democratic presidential nomination in 1960, and he gathered a group of advisers, later known as the "Irish Mafia," who proved to be brilliant strategists. Second, Kefauver's success in 1956 vividly demonstrated to John Kennedy the political advantage of the extensive television exposure Kefauver had gained when he investigated organized crime. Kennedy concluded that to win the presidency, he must establish himself as an

effective legislator by authoring an important piece of legislation and he should also try to obtain national exposure
by participating in an important investigation. He was a
member of the Senate Labor Committee and chose to
make labor legislation his area of expertise during the next
four years. In the process, he became very knowledgeable
in the complicated field of labor law.[8]

His brother Robert had been counsel for the Senate
Committee on Government Operations for several years.
This committee had grown out of the Truman Committee
that examined the government's procurement programs
during World War II. After 1952 the committee's new
chairman, Republican Joe McCarthy of Wisconsin, had
used the investigating committee as a vehicle in his witch-
hunting for subversives in government. Robert Kennedy
and Senator McCarthy were alike in many ways. Both were
Roman Catholic, tough, aggressive, and politically astute.
Robert Kennedy admired McCarthy but disliked his two
chief assistants, counsel Roy Cohn and investigator David
Schine, and finally resigned in protest over Cohn's tactics
in conducting hearings. He undoubtedly was relieved when
Senator John McClellan, Democrat from Arkansas, replaced McCarthy as chairman of both the Committee on
Government Operations and the Subcommittee on Investigations after the Democrats captured control of Congress
in 1954. Robert Kennedy again became counsel for the
committee. McClellan described himself as a hard-shell
Baptist who believed in "foot washing, saving your seed
potatoes and paying your honest debts." He was an important member of the conservative coalition in Congress.
Under McClellan's guidance the committee avoided the
spectacular headline-hunting antics of McCarthy and quietly went about its work. Robert Kennedy soon developed
great admiration and respect for his boss.[9]

Robert Kennedy spent a month working for the Stevenson campaign, then returned to the McClellan Committee.
Soon after the election of 1956 he found himself on the

West Coast for what proved to be the beginning of a major investigation of organized crime's infiltration of the labor union movement. He was greatly assisted by a number of journalists who had been investigating this subject for several years. Clark Mollenhoff, a lawyer and an aggressive reporter for the Cowles Publications, who was probing conditions in Minneapolis, would receive a Pulitzer Prize in 1958 for his reporting. William Lambert was actively investigating in the Northwest, and Pierre Salinger in San Francisco was writing a series on union racketeering for *Collier's*. They were all finding the teamsters to be a rich source of corruption throughout the nation.

In 1956 Clark Mollenhoff began a campaign to convince Robert Kennedy to examine corruption in labor unions. Kennedy believed that jurisdiction over this topic fell under the purview of the Labor Committee rather than Government Operations. Mollenhoff persisted and, as he put it, "taunted him by questioning his courage to take on such an investigation." Stung by this remark, Kennedy decided to explore labor union activities on the West Coast. He was accompanied on this exploratory trip by Carmine Bellino. They talked to a jukebox operator in Los Angeles who was also a labor organizer, who told them a frightening story of intimidation. The organizer had been warned to stay out of the San Diego area or be killed. He went anyway and was knocked unconscious. When he awoke he had terrible pains in his lower abdomen. He managed to reach a hospital, where surgeons extracted a large cucumber. He was informed that the next time he invaded that territory he would receive a watermelon implant. He never returned.[10]

The two investigators moved on to Portland. There they discovered that Frank Brewster, who had replaced Dave Beck as president of the Western Teamsters when the latter became international president, enjoyed horse racing and was illegally using union funds to support his stable of horses. They also heard rumors about Nathan Shefferman, who ran a "labor relations" firm with offices in Chicago, Detroit, and New York City that was actually a union-busting agency, and there was evidence of his direct ties to Dave Beck. Flying to Chicago, they subpoenaed Shefferman's records and pieced together a story of Shefferman's purchases for Beck that ran into thousands of dollars and had been reimbursed with teamster funds. They also found that teamster funds had built Beck's home in Seattle; he then sold the house to the teamsters for $136,000, and the union allowed him to live in it rent free. In a word, they discovered that the president of the nation's largest union, the man who had recently been photographed in a meeting with Republican President Dwight Eisenhower and was to represent his country at an international meeting, was a crook who had embezzled over $350,000 from his union.[11]

Robert Kennedy discussed his findings with McClellan. The senator, though interested in exposing union corruption, responded that this area lay beyond his committee's jurisdiction. A short time later Robert Kennedy checked with the National Labor Relations Board about union reports. The Taft-Hartley Act required unions to make annual financial reports to the Department of Labor. Kennedy was curious about how thoroughly these documents were checked by the Labor Department or the NLRB and wondered if they might give evidence of fiscal wrongdoing. He "was shocked to find that only in rare cases were these statements examined by anyone." They were considered confidential and therefore not open to the public. In fact, the NLRB interpreted the law to mean the records did not have to be accurate; they just had to be filed. Because the reports had to be filed with a government agency, Kennedy and McClellan then reasoned, they were under the jurisdiction of the Government Operations Committee, which oversaw activities of government agencies.[12]

George Meany adamantly opposed proceeding with this investigation until Kennedy convinced him that he had evidence to prove Dave Beck was crooked. Thus, in January 1957, despite Beck's "bellowing opposition," Meany persuaded his executive council to cooperate with the investigation. But Meany considered McClellan "an antilabor nut" and wanted John Kennedy's Labor Committee to take charge. McClellan, remembering that too many labor probes had fizzled in the past, objected that Kennedy's committee was "traditionally gentle." The Senate solved the jurisdictional dispute by creating a special Select Committee on Improper Activities in the Labor-Management Field, which became popularly known as the rackets committee or McClellan Committee. It was to be composed of four senators from Government Operations and four from the Labor Committee. Thus, in addition to McClellan as chairman, Sam Ervin of North Carolina, Joe McCarthy, and Karl Mundt from Government Operations and John Kennedy, Patrick McNamara, Democrat from Michigan, Irving Ives, and Republican Barry Goldwater of Arizona, from the Labor Committee were named to the select committee. The committee thus included three prolabor senators, Kennedy, McNamara, and Ives, and five senators who, if not antilabor, were certainly promanagement.[13]

Joseph Kennedy implored his son not to serve on the committee because he was certain it would turn out to be an antiunion investigation, and such activity could derail his presidential aspirations. The father also insisted that Robert Kennedy not continue as chief counsel, but to no avail. John Kennedy wanted the national exposure, and he later said "Bobby" wanted him on the committee for balance. If John had declined to serve, J. Strom Thurmond, Democrat from South Carolina, was next in line, and "you can imagine what would have happened with Thurmond thrown in with McClellan and Ervin"—and McCarthy, Goldwater, and Mundt. The alcoholic McCarthy took little part in the subsequent hearings and died that same year. Carl Curtis, Republican from Nebraska and an antilabor senator, replaced him. When Ives retired in 1959, he was replaced by Homer Capehart, an antilabor Republican from Indiana, and Mundt became the committee vice-chairman.[14]

Robert Kennedy began assembling a staff. He brought in
Kenneth O'Donnell, his roommate and football teammate
from Harvard days, and hired Pierre Salinger when *Collier's* ceased publication before his series on union corruption was published. Walter Sheridan, a former FBI agent,
also became an important investigator. In addition, Kennedy consistently consulted with investigative reporters,
who provided information, tips about possible witnesses,
and potential areas of investigation. The staff eventually
numbered 104, and the committee heard 1,526 witnesses
during 270 days of public hearings; of these, 343 pleaded
the Fifth Amendment. The staff and committee members
traveled over 2.5 million miles and produced 20,432 pages
of testimony. From its earliest hearings, Robert Kennedy
and John McClellan made certain that the investigations
were thorough, but, unlike the McCarthy Committee, witnesses would receive fair treatment and due process of law.
Of course, there were many who criticized Kennedy for
harassing witnesses when he knew they were not telling
the truth. As Robert Kennedy noted, he never asked a witness a question to which he did not already know the correct answer.[15]

The investigation of Beck proceeded swiftly—as soon as
Beck was found. He was in Europe preparing to represent
the United States in an upcoming International Labor
Organization conference when the committee was ready to
call him. Secretary of Labor Mitchell discussed the committee's evidence on Beck with McClellan and within an
hour called George Meany to inform him he was with-
drawing Beck as the U.S. representative. When Beck returned from Europe and was subpoenaed, it was discovered
that most of his records had been destroyed. But Jimmy
Hoffa, hoping to use Robert Kennedy to bring about Beck's
downfall so he could become international president, was
feeding the chief counsel information, and, through various witnesses, Kennedy produced a solid case that stood up
in court. Even though Beck pleaded the Fifth Amendment
sixty-five times, Kennedy established that, among oth-

er nefarious activities, the union president had taken $370,000 from the Western Conference of Teamsters, that he had given over $85,000 in union funds to Nathan Shefferman for Beck's personal purchases, and that he had arranged a $1.5 million loan from teamster welfare funds for the Fruehauf Trailer Company, which had helped Beck arrange a $200,000 personal loan. Beck eventually was convicted of larceny and income tax evasion, sentenced to prison, and in 1975 received a full pardon from President Gerald Ford. Jimmy Hoffa replaced Beck as president of the teamsters. Hoffa was not only a greater menace to the union movement than Beck because of his aggressive personality and philosophy, but also, unlike Beck, he was allied with criminals and stimulated the movement of organized crime into the labor movement.[16]

Jimmy Hoffa grew up with the teamster movement. Short, stocky, with powerful arms and legs, Hoffa was always ready to use muscles or wits to come out on top. He once claimed he could do seven pushups on the fingertips of one hand. George Meany thought he had a "gangster mentality." Starting out in Detroit, Hoffa soon gained control of the Central States Conference of Teamsters. He then began to spread out, making contacts on the East Coast. Soon Johnny Diogardino (Johnny Dio), a convicted extortionist from New York, became one of his cohorts, as did Tony "Ducks" Corallo, another racketeer from the Empire State. These two men received numerous charters for local teamsters unions and staffed them with former convicts. Johnny Dio was named a regional director of teamsters, and he and his henchmen, parading as labor organizers, negotiated "sweetheart" contracts with small businessmen in New York City. Their members were mostly blacks and Puerto Ricans who paid initiation fees and monthly dues and, in return, received minimum wages and no fringe benefits.[17]

As malfeasance in teamsters unions was being disclosed, many people asked the obvious question, Why did the membership put up with such shenanigans? The answer

lay in the way Hoffa and his cohorts operated and can be il-
lustrated by what happened in LaSalle, Illinois. Barney Matual had formed a local union there and helped three other
locals organize in nearby cities. One day they were visited
by Jimmy Hoffa, Paul Dorfman of Chicago, the Kansas
City teamster boss Roy Williams, the St. Louis boss Dick
Cavner, and three brothers from Joliet, one of whom, Virgil
Floyd, had been convicted of extortion. Dorfman and Jack
Ruby, who later killed Lee Harvey Oswald (the alleged as-
sassin of John Kennedy), controlled a major teamster local
in Chicago. The group announced that the four local inde-
pendents were merging with Virgil Floyd's union. The four
locals, however, voted 694 to 7 against the merger.

Some time later, the four locals voted to merge to present a consolidated front against the pressure from the Illinois teamsters. Floyd and his men then began harassing
employers under contract with Matual's local. President
Dave Beck sent a letter placing the local in trusteeship.
The local members voted overwhelmingly against trusteeship so the international sent an auditor who moved into
the local office and confiscated the cash in the safe. Matual
had the locks changed on the office and placed the local's
bank account in a trust account so the auditor could not
get at it. Hoffa's henchmen then set up a rival local and began trying to raid members through intimidation, and Matual's local affiliated with the United Mine Workers for
protection. The teamsters international then bribed a company official to recognize the rival teamsters local. When
his workers struck in protest, strikebreakers were imported
and the strike was crushed. This was how democracy operated in the teamsters: intimidation, bribery, misuse of
trusteeship, and collusion with management.[18]

Misuse of trusteeships in the teamsters was widespread.
The principle of trusteeship is an excellent one: when a local has serious financial difficulties, poor leadership, or
other problems, the international places it in the hands of
a trustee, who takes the necessary steps to restore it to

good standing. But too often the local "problem" was opposition to Hoffa's leadership, and his solution was appointment of one of his lieutenants as trustee until the
local was restored to good standing by complying with
Hoffa's policy. Occasionally the reverse took place. A character named Connelly drained his local's treasury in Minneapolis and was replaced by a trustee. Hoffa soon fired the
trustee and reinstated Connelly as the local leader even
though he was under indictment for extortion and dyna-
miting. Although the teamsters paid $54,000 in legal fees
to defend him, Connelly was convicted and imprisoned. In
1957, 12 percent of teamsters locals were in trusteeship.
As Senator McClellan noted, trusteeships were "usually . . . being used by the international as cloaks for dis-
honesty, corruption, and the quelling of honest insurgency
by the decent rank and file members."[19]

Another obvious question was why the rank and file did
not run for office and clean up their local. The answer lay
in teamster rules. Only members who paid their dues by
the first of the month were eligible for office. Members
were on the checkoff system, and their dues arrived after
the first of the month. Only officers paid their dues person-
ally and before the due date so they usually ran unopposed
for their offices.[20]

Soon after the McClellan Committee's investigation of
Jimmy Hoffa's activities began, John Cye Cheasty approached Robert Kennedy with an intriguing story. Hoffa
had hired him as a spy to obtain a job with the committee
as an investigator. Cheasty, an honest man, subsequently
agreed to work with the FBI as a double agent and began
passing selected information to Hoffa. The FBI sprang its
trap by catching Cheasty passing Hoffa an envelope of information and Hoffa giving him $2,000 in payment. The
FBI then arrested Hoffa on charges of bribery and conspiracy. In June 1957 Hoffa went on trial. Robert Kennedy
described the case as so airtight that if Hoffa was not convicted he would "jump off the Capitol."[21]

Hoffa was defended brilliantly by Edward Bennett Williams and prosecuted weakly by the U.S. attorney. Williams had been attorney for Beck and, among others, Frank Costello, an underworld figure. Hoffa took the witness stand and defended his actions by contending that he had hired Cheasty in good faith as a lawyer and naturally accepted any documents his counsel gave him. There was no intent to bribe, Hoffa argued. He had hired Cheasty before the committee did; therefore, the committee corrupted his lawyer, not the reverse.

Williams questioned Cheasty's integrity on the witness stand by demanding an accounting of the money Hoffa had given him. Cheasty did so but admitted he had given his wife $20 of it to buy shoes for his children, and the seed of doubt was sown in the jurors' minds. Williams also charged that Cheasty had been opposed to the National Association for the Advancement of Colored People (NAACP) in an investigation of a Tallahassee dispute over bus integration.

Government counsel was careless in the selection of the jury. Several of the jurors had police records, one had a son who was in jail on a narcotics charge, and one had lost his government job because he had failed to pass a lie detector test. Two-thirds of the jury were black. During the trial the *Afro-American*, a Washington, D.C., black newspaper, carried a story headlined "The Facts Behind the Hoffa Trial." The account called McClellan and the trial judge racial bigots and praised Hoffa and Edward Bennett Williams as champions of civil rights. Hoffa's Teamsters, it noted, had "167,000 colored truck drivers." The newspaper was delivered to all the jurors. Shortly thereafter, Joe Louis, the former world champion boxer, appeared in the courtroom. He and Hoffa grabbed each other by the arms and engaged in an animated conversation in front of the jury. Louis immediately became a public relations consultant for the Mercury Record Company in Chicago, and one of the company's officers received a $2 million loan from the teamster pension fund. The jury acquitted Hoffa. A few days later, the McClellan Committee announced a major investigation of the teamsters.

Jimmy Hoffa was not worried. He had been investigated several times before, and he could predict the scenerio. Witnesses would be called, little of substance would be proved, and the investigation would stall, then be abandoned from lack of interest. He did not count on the relentless Robert Kennedy. During the next three years of investigations and later as attorney general, Kennedy pursued Hoffa's activities in what many described as a "vendetta." He considered the labor leader and his power over American transportation a menace to the country and his financial abuses of the rank and file an abomination. Hoffa, in turn, considered Kennedy an upstart, a spoiled millionaire, a parasite on society. Kennedy recalled that during the hearings "Hoffa would stare fixedly at me, not blinking, for a long time, maybe as long as ten minutes, and then without warning he would close one eye in a mischievous wink. It was really disconcerting."[22]

The hearings began with a patronizing Hoffa calling Kennedy "Bobby" and discussing union philosophy with the Republican senators.

Senator Mundt: Basically, do you believe in socialism?
Mr. Hoffa: I positively do not.
Senator Mundt: Do you believe in our private enterprise system?
Mr. Hoffa: I certainly do.
Senator Mundt: Is there some difference in political philosophy between you and some other prominent labor leaders in this country?
Mr. Hoffa: Well, there certainly is, and it is going to remain so. . . . I believe that management and labor very definitely must at all times have something in common because one without the other cannot survive.
Senator Mundt: I must agree with you on that statement 100 percent.[23]

Kennedy began his interrogation of Hoffa with Hoffa's friendship with Johnny Diogardino. Hoffa's lieutenants pleaded the Fifth Amendment when they testified, but he was determined not to do so and relied instead on a faulty memory. As Kennedy doggedly quizzed him, using legally recorded telephone conversations, Hoffa lost his self-confidence. At one point, in response to a question, he said, "To the best of my recollection, I must recall on my memory, I cannot remember." Kennedy responded that Hoffa "had the worst case of amnesia . . . that I ever heard of." As the hearings ground on into 1959, Hoffa developed a new technique. He repeatedly denied certain testimony that had been given, thus killing much time in locating and rereading the questioned record.[24]

The committee uncovered case after case of questionable loans of money that had been made to Hoffa. He had "borrowed" thousands of dollars at no interest from Jack Buskin, a labor relations adviser in Detroit, J.L. Keeshin, a Chicago truck line operator, and Henry Lower, promoter of a Florida real estate project with which Hoffa was connected and was promoting to rank-and-file teamster members. This Sun Valley real estate venture was also financed by an interest-free deposit of $400,000 from Hoffa's Detroit local that served as collateral for a $395,000 loan from an Orlando bank. In turn, Hoffa helped Lower borrow $75,000 at a low interest rate from a Detroit bank in which Hoffa kept teamster money. Hoffa's local loaned $75,000 to the Marberry Construction Company, owned by Herbert Grosberg, a teamster accountant, and George Fitzgerald, a teamster attorney. Hoffa, in turn, received an $11,500 loan from Grosberg. There were many instances when Hoffa hired convicted criminals as business agents or placed them in charge of trusteeships. The hearings uncovered a nationwide network of underworld connections with the teamsters.[25]

Meanwhile, in October 1957 the teamsters elected Jimmy Hoffa to replace Dave Beck as international president. To the rank and file, Hoffa was the perfect teamster: tough, always ready to fight for his rights, a martyr to the teamster cause because of Kennedy's abusive treatment, a leader who fought for better wages and fringe benefits for his members. They raised his salary to $50,000 per year and voted the convicted Beck a large annual pension.

As these revelations of corruption in unions surfaced in the 1950s, Walter Reuther reminded George Meany that the CIO had expelled its communist-controlled unions and now it was time for him to clean up the corrupt AFL-affiliated unions. Meany persuaded the AFL-CIO executive council to adopt a strict code of conduct for its affiliates, and, when Dave Beck pleaded the Fifth Amendment during his hearings, the AFL-CIO expelled him from the council. With the further revelations of the McClellan Committee in the Hoffa hearings, the AFL-CIO expelled the teamsters during the convention in 1957. Hoffa then began to seek ties with Harry Bridges's West Coast longshoremen, who had been ousted from the CIO for being dominated by communists, and the East Coast longshoremen, who had been expelled for failing to clean up corruption.[26]

To carry Hoffa's tale beyond the present story, Attorney General Robert Kennedy pursued his nemesis into the 1960s. In April 1964 Hoffa and seven codefendants were charged with conspiracy to defraud the teamsters pension fund. That July a jury found Hoffa guilty on all four counts, and he was sentenced to five years in prison in addition to his eight-year sentence in March 1964 for jury tampering in a Tennessee trial. Hoffa continued as teamster president while in jail until he resigned in December 1971. Frank Fitzsimmons was then elected president of the teamsters, and President Richard Nixon immediately granted Hoffa a conditional pardon. The condition he attached was that Hoffa could not serve as a union official before 6 March 1980. Questions arose about enforcement of this condition, and Hoffa began discussing running for office. In July 1975 he disappeared without a trace. The mystery still has not been solved, and many people assumed that he was murdered by criminal elements.

The McClellan Committee, which by this time was popularly known as the rackets committee, did not devote all its attention to the teamsters, although thirty-four of the fifty-eight volumes of testimony were related to that union. Robert Kennedy discovered that James G. Cross, president of the bakery and confectionery workers had changed his union's constitution to make him a virtual dictator. In their convention in 1956 the members amended their constitution to provide for election of officers at the annual convention rather than by the entire membership and abolished the use of *Robert's Rules of Order* to govern their procedures. Cross was empowered to decide where union funds were to be deposited, and his salary and that of the secretary-treasurer were to be set by the executive council rather than the full convention. The executive council immediately nearly doubled his salary, which favor he reciprocated by giving the board members a hefty raise. In addition, he was spending thousands of dollars of union funds annually for "entertainment" such as a family trip to London and Paris and for maintaining a mistress. The AFL-CIO then ousted the bakers union.[27]

The McClellan Committee also investigated the operating engineers and the carpenters unions. Joey Fay, a racketeer–labor official in New Jersey and Pennsylvania, was convicted for shaking down employers for over $700,000. His union paid his legal fees ($63,000) and gave him a handsome pension. Officers of the San Francisco branch of operating engineers spent $120,000 in union funds for a yacht and an airplane. They remained in power by stuffing the ballot boxes. Any opposition to their rule brought beatings and, in at least one case, death. The president reported an income of $388,000 from 1950 to 1956, a figure that was actually short by $354,000. Much of this difference came from double and triple expense payments. After the McClellan Committee exposed these activities, he resigned and received a $50,000 annual pension.

Charley Johnson, vice-president of the carpenters union,

was involved with Hoffa in an Indiana land development scheme. Hoffa had asked Cye Cheasty to find out if the McClellan Committee had any evidence of Johnson's wrongdoing. The committee knew that from 1955 to 1957 he received $450,000 from the carpenters union while at the same time he was part owner and salesman for Penn Products. Ninety percent of his annual income of $96,000 from the Penn company from 1950 to 1957 came from purchases by construction companies that needed his goodwill as an officer in the carpenters union. Their dealings with him, in effect, were payoffs. Anthony Valente and Lloyd Klenert, president and secretary-treasurer of the United Textile Workers Union, used union funds to purchase luxury homes. They explained that they were merely "hiding" the money so no one could steal it.[28]

It has often been overlooked that the McClellan Committee not only made shocking revelations about corruption and organized crime among labor leaders and their thousands of lawyers but also found collusion among employers. The committee had no jurisdiction to investigate business in general but could check into situations that involved labor-management relations. The committee found more than fifty corporations and companies that had acted illegally in their dealings with unions. They were ignoring the Taft-Hartley Act with impunity, in some cases as a result of threats or intimidation and in others for pecuniary gain. S.A. Healy, owner of a large construction firm, had given "Big Mike" Carozza of the hod carriers union $125,000 as a payoff.

Several newspapers across the country were involved in shakedowns. Harry Gross was a convicted extortionist who was president of a teamsters local in Florida. Robert Kennedy found that the Neo-Gravure Company of New Jersey had paid Gross $1,000 per month following his release from Sing Sing to ensure labor peace. In 1948 a teamsters strike in New York City halted newspaper distribution, except for the *New York Times* and the *New*

York Daily Mirror, whose Sunday magazines were printed by the Neo-Gravure Company. The *Times* paid $35,000 and the *Mirror* $10,000 to Gross to get the papers delivered. The *Detroit Times* was involved in a similar shakedown.[29]

The Nathan Shefferman labor relations firm had an unusual product to sell: it was a union-busting business. The McClellan Committee was criticized for stressing corruption in unions so the Shefferman hearings provided an important balance. Nathan Shefferman was labor relations manager for Sears, Roebuck & Company until 1948, when he reached mandatory retirement age. From then on he served as a consultant for Sears. As a result of his efforts, in 1958 only 14,000 of the company's 205,000 employees belonged to a union, and half of those organized belonged to the teamsters. Shefferman had about three hundred other clients; twenty-eight of the largest of these used his firm for breaking their unions. Part of the success of his company lay with his ties to Dave Beck. The McClellan Committee found that the company had spawned a number of phony company unions for Sears in Boston, the Whirlpool plants in Ohio, Allstate Insurance (Sears) in Michigan, and the Englander Company in Chicago. The Morton Frozen Foods Company had paid Shefferman $12,000 in 1956 for keeping a union out and paid him $8,000 the following year for bringing in a company union. As Daniel Bell described it, the Shefferman findings created "a tale that has given business its worst publicity since the days of the La Follette hearings twenty years ago."[30]

In 1955 Food Fair Stores, one of the largest food chains in the nation, created an affiliate that made "stock rights" available to certain people. Four were union officials, including Max and Louis Block of the meat cutters union. In return, Food Fair was granted an eighteen-month period of grace before having to pay into the union pension fund and welfare fund. The chain made its stock available at a cheap price to Ben Lapensohn of the teamsters and, in turn, was granted a $300,000 advantage over its competitors in the next contract with respect to the unloading of merchandise. When the CIO retail clerks union negotiated a forty-hour workweek with Safeway, a large grocery chain, A&P (the Great Atlantic and Pacific Tea Company, a competitor) gave Max Block ten thousand of its organized workers in return for a five-year contract for a forty-five-hour workweek. The company saved $2 million per year, and the union received $500,000 per year in dues. The A&P attorney told the McClellan Committee he "did not see anything wrong with it."[31]

Meanwhile, in an attempt to divert the committee's interest away from himself, Jimmy Hoffa and his cohorts successfully launched a whispering campaign, warning Republican members of the committee that if the teamsters union was crushed, Walter Reuther of the UAW would move in and organize teamster members. Although the Republican senators did not approve of Hoffa's methods, he was a staunch supporter of the Republican party and Reuther was an arch-liberal Democrat, whom some of them believed to be a greater threat to the United States than any other labor leader.

Like Hoffa, Reuther began union organizing early in his life. Walter and his brother Victor traveled to the Soviet Union when they were youths, living and working in a factory in Gorki. It was at that time, in 1934, that "Vic and Wal" supposedly wrote their famous letter to an American friend praising the Russian economic system and urging him to "carry on the fight." Both brothers returned to the United States and in the strife-torn automobile industry participated in the sit-down strikes and accompanying violence associated with the UAW during the Great Depression. During the strike at Flint, Michigan, mimeographed copies of the Gorki letter were distributed with the ending altered to read "Carry on the fight for a Soviet America." This letter went through several editions, and Clare Hoffman inserted two different versions of it in the *Congressional Record.*[32]

Walter Reuther eventually became president of the

UAW and, later, of the CIO. Walter Reuther and Jimmy Hoffa had a common background in labor violence, but there the resemblance ended. Unlike Hoffa, Reuther accepted a small salary and was dedicated to promoting the welfare of his union members and the good of American society. But conservatives viewed with alarm his liberal views as well as his immense power in organized labor. When Joe McCarthy died in 1957, Senator Carl Curtis, Republican from Nebraska, replaced him on the rackets committee. Curtis, Mundt, and Goldwater were determined to bring Reuther down.

Following the lurid teamsters hearings and the tamer investigation of the bakers union, the McClellan Committee "seemed to slow down." The Republican members of the committee, *Newsweek* reported, were certain the committee was "being involved, indirectly if not directly, in maneuvering for the next Democratic Presidential nomination." The GOP members argued that the committee's sharpest attacks were directed at those who stood "in the way of Reuther's domination of American labor." Senator Goldwater proclaimed publicly that Reuther and the UAW "have done more damage and violence to freedom than was accomplished by all the peculiar financial transactions of Mr. Dave Beck." Karl Mundt answered a correspondent with the observation that "murder and the beating of American citizens by labor goons [of the CIO] is even worse than the loose fiscal policies engaged in by the Becks and by Jimmy Hoffa."[33]

Senator Mundt was also critical of the way McClellan and Robert Kennedy were conducting their investigation. It was largely a two-person affair, and committee members often had no idea what investigations were under way until they read of them in a newspaper or heard about them in the committee hearing room. Mundt believed that it was "unfortunate" that Senator John Kennedy was apparently a candidate for the Democratic presidential nomination and was "consequently perhaps less likely to want to tackle the question of improper practices in the mighty UMW . . . and Reuther." Mundt asked McClellan and Robert Kennedy to appoint two "associate counsels," one of whom was to be in Washington, D.C., at all times so that committee members could consult with him and exercise more control over committee proceedings. This request resulted in an acrimonious meeting of the committee on 15 July 1957, at which time committee procedures were altered to accommodate the South Dakota senator's demands. Mundt described the new guidelines as "contructive and correct" and issued a press release describing the meeting as "completely harmonious."[34]

Robert Kennedy liked and admired Senators Ives and Goldwater but disliked Curtis and considered Mundt "a sanctimonious hypocrite who played up to Reuther and Hoffa while they were on the witness seat and attacked them viciously" at other times. Much to Kennedy's irritation, Mundt constantly leaked committee business to the press, although Kennedy occasionally did the same thing. Kennedy and Salinger confirmed their suspicions once by sending each of the senators a different copy of a draft report. Mundt's version soon appeared in the newspapers. As a member of the McClellan Committee, Mundt was convinced that "the most important 'racket' we can expose is the relationship of union power and union money to our body politic." He wrote Raymond Moley, a *Newsweek* columnist, that the Republicans were "keeping a sharp eye" on their general counsel. "I believe in the final analysis," Mundt wrote, "he will aid us in exposing whatever derogatory evidence becomes available on Mr. Reuther's activities." Mundt and Goldwater especially wanted to investigate Reuther's activities in the current bitter UAW strike against the Kohler Company.[35]

The local union of Kohler workers affiliated with the UAW in October 1952. This was not an unreasonable affiliation because, although Kohler manufactured bathroom appliances, it also had a motor division. The follow-

ing March the UAW signed a one-year contract with
Kohler. In February 1954 the union asked for a $.20 per
hour raise ($.10 for skilled workers), a union shop, a hos-
pital plan, and a $137.50 per month pension plan. When
the owner and management, which were violently antiunion, offered only a $.03 raise and no fringe benefits, the
union struck. By August the union was willing to settle for
$.10 ($.05 for skilled workers), but the company, determined to break the union, refused and began hiring nonunion workers. A long strike ensued with dynamite and
shotguns dividing the citizens of Sheboygan, Wisconsin. In
April 1956 the national UAW had to stop strike payments,
which had cost $10 million to that point with no end in
sight. Finally, in 1957 a group of local clergymen sought to
mediate the dispute, but Kohler refused to rehire 192 of the
most active leaders, and the union supported the strikers.
Mundt, convinced that communists were behind the violence, received an FBI report on the leading strikers and the
Reuthers and a copy of the Gorki letter they had written
from Russia in 1934 to use as evidence against the UAW.[36]

Robert Kennedy agreed to send Jack McGovern to investigate the strike. He did not think that anything would be
uncovered that the NLRB hearings had not already exposed
but decided that this would satisfy the Republicans because McGovern had been hired at Goldwater's request. At
this point Goldwater reported that he was as "happy as a
squirrel in a little cage," and Mundt said he was "as happy
as a South Dakota pheasant in a South Dakota cornfield."
During the next few months McGovern did not report to
Kennedy but corresponded frequently with the Republicans. Mundt asked him to report to his Madison, South
Dakota, office. Finally, McGovern sent McClellan a
memorandum that, according to Robert Kennedy, was substantially a copy of the NLRB report minus any "derogatory" information about the company. *Fortune* magazine
observed that it was "clear that McGovern intends to
show that the UAW is using its enormous financial re-

sources in a 'vindictive' manner against a company that
has replaced striking workers and has continued to operate
despite a boycott." Robert Kennedy was in a bad spot. He
was convinced that if the committee investigated the
strike, it would find nothing the NLRB had not already revealed, but if he did not proceed, critics would believe he
was avoiding an investigation to encourage the UAW to
support his brother in 1960. When the Republicans persisted in their demands for an investigation, Kennedy decided to visit Sheboygan.[37]

His visit, he said, reminded him of his trip to the Middle
East and the hatred he had felt there between Jew and
Arab. "Unless you can see and feel for yourself the agony
that has shattered this Wisconsin community," he reported, "it is difficult to believe that such a concentration
of hatred can exist in this country." He toured the enamel
shop, where the oven heat was intense and workers were
given only a short lunch break. The UAW had asked for a
thirty-minute lunch period but was told this was unnecessary. Kennedy thought the company attorney was rabidly
antiunion. On the other side, citizens told him stories of
violence done to themselves or family members by strikers. He interviewed the UAW officials and decided they
could defend their case if hearings were held.[38]

At an executive session held on 8 January 1958, Senator
John Kennedy moved that the UAW-Kohler hearings be the
next order of business. Shortly before the hearings began,
McGovern, at the direction of Senator Mundt, approached
Russell Nixon, a former Harvard professor, with a request
that he give information about the alleged communist
leanings of UAW officials. This and the Reuther brothers'
letter from Gorki were to serve as the basis for the Republican attack. But when Nixon made this strategy public,
the plan fell through. In an executive session to plan the
hearings, McGovern proposed that Lyman Conger, the
company's attorney, be called as the first company witness
and that a minor official speak for the UAW. Robert Ken-

nedy responded by suggesting that Walter Reuther be the first UAW witness. This "stirred up so much bitterness among the members that many questioned whether we could ever work together again." The Republican committee members insisted that Reuther could not be the first UAW witness. After they threatened to walk out of the committee, McClellan capitulated to their demand.[39]

The hearings began with Robert Kennedy questioning Conger about the enamel shop. Conger defended the two- to five-minute lunch break on the grounds that the workers had been "doing it for thirty-six years." The UAW official in charge of the strike, Emil Mazey, was called. He proved to be a belligerent witness, who, as Kennedy put it, "shouted first and thought later" and made a poor impression for his union. The first few days of hearings on the Kohler strike were filled with strong recriminations on both sides and prompted Reuther to write Barry Goldwater a well-publicized letter. At a fund-raising dinner in Detroit in January 1958 the senator had made the serious charge that "Walter Reuther and the UAW are a more dangerous menace than the sputniks or anything Russia might do." Reuther pleaded for "sanity" in the Kohler hearings, and he offered Goldwater a challenge: they should each select three prominent clergymen to serve as a panel to hear the senator's charges and Reuther's response. If a majority of the panel then believed the charges were substantiated, Reuther would resign from all his offices in the labor movement. Three days later Goldwater responded that this was a "public relations gimmick." He noted that the Sheboygan clergymen had denounced the UAW and the labor violence that occurred during the strike, and "the irresponsible exercise of power" by Reuther and the UAW officials demonstrated that they "constitute an important danger to our democratic institutions."[40]

Following Mazey's acrimonious testimony, especially after he accused all of Sheboygan's clergymen of being controlled by the Kohler Company, Senator Goldwater

repeated comments about a Democratic "coverup" and
now saw no reason for Reuther to testify. But Kennedy persisted, and Reuther proved more than able to defend himself before his Republican critics. He "seized the
initiative" by accusing Curtis, Goldwater, and Mundt of
"digging for political pay dirt" and said "they would get
more votes if they showed some concern for the plight of
the unemployed, the problems of farmers, schools and hospital needs."[41]

Reuther had earlier asked Robert Kennedy to send an investigator to check his and Mrs. Reuther's personal fi-
nances, which was done before he testified to the
McClellan Committee. The UAW financial records were
also examined, of course, and Carmine Bellino informed
the committee that UAW records were well kept and there
was no indication of misuse or misappropriation of union
funds by Walter Reuther. On the last day of the hearings,
even Senator Mundt told Reuther that "there is no evidence before us of corruption so far as your activities are
concerned." Goldwater admitted to Robert Kennedy that
he was correct and said, "this investigation was not one in
which we should have become involved." Senator Mc-
Clellan observed that the Kohler hearing cost $50,000 and
was "a most fruitless" investigation.[42]

This was the last public hearing held by the committee.
Robert Kennedy soon resigned to write a book about his
rackets committee experience. One day while writing he
heard that Goldwater had told the press that Kennedy "had
run out on the Reuther investigation." Enraged, he tele-
phoned the Arizona senator and demanded an explanation.
"That's politics," Goldwater answered. Kennedy replied
that he considered the McClellan Committee to be bipartisan and he "had tried to run the investigation on nonpo-
litical lines." Goldwater's curt response was "You're in
politics, Bob, whether you like it or not."[43]

The rackets investigation had several important results.
Robert Kennedy received national coverage as a relentless

investigator who, many believed, was dedicated to exposing corruption in unions and many others thought often
crossed the line into a form of McCarthyism in his zealous
questioning of recalcitrant witnesses. His brother John
would use the hearings to his advantage in seeking the
Democratic presidential nomination in 1960. So too would
Barry Goldwater in his quest for the Republican presidential nomination in 1964. Before the hearings began,
Reuther and other labor leaders viewed John Kennedy as "a
lightweight opportunist." But his conduct during the Kohler hearings and his efforts to secure passage of labor legislation in 1958 and 1959 "brought a complete turnabout in
their attitude." They would support him in 1960 instead of
their former favorites, Adlai Stevenson and Hubert
Humphrey.[44]

The hearings proved that Dave Beck, Jimmy Hoffa, and
many teamsters officials were corrupt and that organized
crime had infiltrated the labor movement. Their defense
was that two decades earlier management had used criminals in the fight against unions and now the hoodlums
were on the other side. But the investigations also showed
that thousands of businessmen and lawyers across the
country had joined corrupt union officials in their nefarious activities. Yet as a result of the hearings, only the AFL-
CIO made an attempt to clean up corruption among its
members. Bar associations sought no disciplinary action
against corrupt lawyers as a result of the McClellan exposures. The National Association of Manufacturers and the
United States Chamber of Commerce took no punitive
action against businessmen exposed as participating in
corrupt labor-management practices. In fact, such businessmen often were accorded hero status and became
models for their antiunion actions.

The McClellan Committee submitted an interim report
in March 1958 and a final report in February 1960. The interim report recommended legislation to regulate pension,
health, and welfare funds; to regulate union funds; to en-

sure union democracy; to curb activities of middlemen
such as Nathan Shefferman in labor-management disputes;
and to clarify the "no-man's-land" in labor-management
relations where both the NLRB and the states refused to
assert jurisdiction. In 1958 Congress moved to control
union pension funds and the following year enacted legislation to carry out the remaining recommendations, plus
many more.[45]

Finally, televising the rackets committee hearings had a
great impact on the American people. To much of the public, "labor" came to be associated with Jimmy Hoffa, and
Hoffa meant arrogance and bossism. Many people concluded that the McClellan Committee had proved that "labor was corrupt" and that "something ought to be done"
about it." The result was a new ambivalence toward
unions. Unions had previously been defended as vehicles
through which workers achieved "some measure of inde-
pendence and dignity" in the workplace and some protection against arbitrary management decisions. After the
rackets committee revelations, the public began to think
that unions also were instruments of labor bosses, especially Jimmy Hoffa and the teamsters, who exploited the
workers and lived in ill-gotten luxury from union funds,
and often concluded that union members had little or no
control over their elected officials. The successful appeal to
the public view that union corruption should be controlled
helped persuade Congress to take action, and the result
was the Landrum-Griffin Act of 1959.[46]

4. Senator Kennedy
Writes a Bill

In April 1954 a subcommittee of the Senate Committee on Labor and Public Welfare began a thorough investigation of the administration of union welfare funds. The Democrats gained control of Congress in the elections of 1954, and Senator Paul Douglas of Illinois chaired the committee in the following year. The committee found many abuses: funds administered solely by the union in violation of the law; employers indifferent to administration of these funds; high administrative costs; low insurance benefits; policies changed by insurance brokers for their own financial benefit; and state and national laws that were inadequate to regulate effectively the administration of these funds. The subcommittee cited the Laundry Workers International as an example. Its welfare fund was to be administered jointly with trustees, but, in fact, the insurance it purchased for members was controlled by Louis J. Saperstein, a New Jersey broker. The Security Mutual Insurance Company was the carrier from April 1950 to September 1953. Normally Saperstein's commission during this period would have been about $35,000. Actually he received $206,507.59. In addition, when the carrier was changed to a California company, he garnered approximately $900,000 by postdating coverage, retaining late payments, and under-reporting the number of members for whom he had received payments.[1]

These investigations, coupled with those of the Senate

rackets committee revelations and the Department of Labor interpretation of Taft-Hartley that union financial reports did not have to be disclosed, demonstrated the need for corrective legislation in this field. But it was not until 1958 that Congress acted. In April of that year the Senate Labor and Public Welfare Committee reported a bill sponsored by Senators Kennedy, Douglas, and Ives. The proposal covered all pension and welfare funds, regardless of who controlled or administered them, but exempted unions with fewer than one hundred employees. The legislation would require annual reports to the secretary of labor, on standardized forms, giving the size of the fund, premiums, fees, contributions, trustees, and other pertinent information. It contained criminal penalties for filing false statements, embezzlement, kickbacks, and destruction of records. It further authorized the secretary of labor to sue to prevent violations or gross mismanagement of funds. Because the proposal covered one of the five recommendations of the McClellan Committee's interim report, Secretary of Labor James Mitchell endorsed the Kennedy-Douglas-Ives bill.[2]

In introducing his legislation, Kennedy called attention to the huge sums these funds involved. They contained at least $30 billion with $7 to 8 billion in annual contributions. More than 75 million workers and their dependents, or more than half the population of the United States, were dependent on these deposits, and only five states made any attempt to regulate them. The Massachusetts senator noted that the *New York Times* on 3 November 1957 estimated that at least $5 million annually was involved in white-collar crime through kickbacks, payoffs, and bribery in administering these funds. This was probably a gross underestimation.[3]

William F. Knowland, an antilabor Republican from California and Senate minority leader, wanted to run for governor of his state in November 1958 and was determined to make labor legislation his primary issue. In Janu-

ary he introduced S. 3068 to provide what he called a labor
bill of rights. His proposal would require a secret ballot in
elections for union officials and for their recall and for any
strike vote. He also wanted to protect union welfare funds,
control trusteeships, and require strict audits of union fees,
dues, and assessments. He testified for his bill before the
Kennedy subcommittee and when the Kennedy-Douglas-
Ives measure was debated in the Senate, he offered his proposal as an amendment. It was rejected because a majority
of the senators thought it would be unfair to labor unions
to approve changes not studied by the committee. Pension
and welfare fund reporting had been investigated for four
years by committees, but not Knowland's specific ideas. As
Senate Majority Leader Lyndon B. Johnson assured George
Meany, he did not want shotgun amendments attached to
this bill until hearings were conducted on them. He noted
that Knowland wanted a roll call vote on the question because he thought forty Republicans supported him. Johnson believed he had thirty-eight or thirty-nine so "we have
to get through to some of them." Either Johnson or labor
leaders did get through because this and other amendments
were defeated.[4]

Lyndon Johnson asked George Reedy, his legislative aide
for labor legislation, to analyze whether Knowland "won"
or "lost" on this labor issue. Reedy admitted that there
was no single answer to this question but thought the Cali-
fornian probably came out behind. He believed Knowland
gained in the newspapers and his name would now be connected with labor reform, and he probably picked up support from farmers, small businessmen, and white-collar
workers. But he definitely lost with union workers. "The
Republican idea that union workers are 'anxious' to be pro-
tected from 'labor bosses' is a myth," Reedy insisted. If
workers were members of a "clean" union they "knew better. If they are members of a 'racketeering' union *the
probabilities are that they are pretty well cared for.*" Usually, he noted, dishonest labor leaders took better care of

their members than honest ones because they "will make side deals that honest men will not consider." Most of the "sell-out" of workers took place in small individual locals, he added, and laborers voted in disregard of their union officials' instructions, but "they won't vote *against* their leaders." If Congress were to enact a labor law in 1958, Reedy concluded, "the issue will die down" and voters would remember only that Senator McClellan *"exposed the racketeers and a Democratic Congress did something about them."*[5]

Several other Republican senators sought to amend the Kennedy-Douglas-Ives bill to include their particular concerns. Goldwater disliked the idea that the regulations would cover all pension and welfare funds. He believed that George Meany wanted these funds to be disclosed so that unions could "whipsaw" industry against industry and business against business, with the result that employees would lose profit-sharing plans. Noting that there already were "too many government regulations," his amendment sought to exempt plans approved by the Internal Revenue Service (IRS)—or profit-sharing plans. The IRS permitted companies to apply 15 percent of their profits to these plans as long as their total did not exceed 25 percent of their total payroll. Kennedy responded to this idea by quoting the IRS commissioner, who had told his committee that his agency was busy collecting revenue and should not be charged with supervising investment plans. The amendment lost.[6]

Other Republicans introduced amendments that would enact the remaining four recommendations of the McClellan Committee. All of these were beaten back by the Democrats on the basis that their inclusion violated the committee system and that the committee would later recommend legislation to address these problems. Kennedy promised specifically to hold hearings on a broad anticorruption bill and bring it to the Senate later that year. Based on this assurance, Senate Majority Leader Lyndon Johnson was able to prevent southern Democrats from bolting the party and joining the Republicans in amending the pension and welfare funds bill.

Goldwater denounced this Democratic opposition by quoting an editorial by David Lawrence in the *Washington Evening Star* that declared that the reason for their resistance was that unions contributed heavily to their campaign chests. This charge brought angry denials, even from Ives and George Aiken, liberal Republican from Vermont, who considered Lawrence's allegation an affront to the integrity of Senator McClellan. Finally, Karl Mundt offered an amendment that would deny convicted felons (defined as those who had been disfranchised by their conviction) from serving as officers, trustees, or custodians for a welfare or pension fund. It passed the Senate by a vote of ninety to zero, and the final bill was approved eighty-eight to zero and sent to the House.[7]

The following July the House approved a much weaker bill and substituted it for the Senate measure. George Meany blamed this substitute on Congressman Ludwig Teller, Democrat from New York, who headed a subcommittee to rewrite the Kennedy-Ives bill. Graham Barden, North Carolina Democrat and chairman of the parent House Committee on Education and Labor, told the subcommittee to take a "fresh look" at the problem. Teller wrote a new bill that considerably watered down the Senate bill, explaining that the Senate measure tried to do "too much." Paul Sifton, a legislative aide for Walter Reuther, explained that Teller's thinking and behavior stemmed from his unusual relationship with Jimmy Hoffa. Sifton sent Reuther a copy of an editorial from the *Washington Daily News* that explained that the close friendship between Hoffa and Teller dated back to 1954, when the congressman got the House Committee on Education and Labor to drop its contempt of Congress charges against the teamster president. Hoffa, of course, was much happier with the weak House bill than the Senate version. Barden then told the Senate to take the House bill or nothing.[8]

The House of Representatives' bill eliminated the provisions for criminal penalties, uniform reporting, and permitting the secretary of labor to sue. Ignoring the telegrams George Meany sent to congressmen asking their support for the Senate version, the House approved its own proposal. When the two houses went to conference, the House managers insisted that their bill be accepted, and they carried the day. The reported bill was basically the House version. The Senate demanded, and received, a uniform report form, but the reporters were not required to use it. The Senate then approved the measure as better than nothing. The law, named the Welfare and Pension Plans Act of 1958, was based on the concept of voluntary self-policing, that is, the unions and their members would regulate the plan. It exempted plans covering twenty-five or fewer people and required that financial information be made available to plan participants. It made falsification or concealment of information a felony, punishable by fines of up to $1,000 and six months in prison.[9]

On 29 August 1958 President Eisenhower reluctantly signed the Welfare and Pension Plans Act into law. He emphasized that it dealt with only a minute part of the problem and failed to provide adequate protection for the funds of almost 85 million workingmen and their dependents. He believed it was "most unrealistic" to rely on individual employees to go to court for enforcement of the law. He signed it only because it established the precedent of federal "responsibility" in this area and noted that "if the bill is to be at all effective, it will require extensive amendment at the next session of Congress."[10]

Eisenhower's statement was the official administration response to the law. Secretary of Labor Mitchell was asked by a newspaper editor to explain the difference between the act that passed and the Senate version that the Eisenhower administration had endorsed. He responded with a copy of the president's statement when he signed the bill and specified that the act did not require uniform reporting forms or detailed financial statements. Mitchell said that

other weaknesses in the law included the omission of the
Senate requirements for criminal penalties and that authorization of the secretary of labor to make rules and
regulations to enforce the law were inadequate, as were the
provisions for investigations and court action to ensure
compliance.[11]

Secretary Mitchell was soon complaining that the law
was not being complied with, and in 1960 he asked Congress for power to control kickbacks, embezzlement, and
similar abuses. But it was not until 1962 that Congress
made any changes in the law. Experience with the act had
shown how easily financial disclosure could be avoided.
Walter Reuther agreed that the law was extremely weak
because it depended on rank-and-file members to report
violations and would have no effect on those who were "perv-
erting employee benefit plans." He recommended that it be
amended to authorize the secretary of labor to establish report forms, to investigate suspected violations, and to require more specific and complete reporting information.
He also thought "enforcement teeth" should be added to
make kickbacks and embezzlement liable to criminal penalties. Adam Clayton Powell, Democrat from New York
and member of the House Committee on Education and
Labor, introduced some minor amendments that became
law. The changes authorized the secretary of labor to pre-
scribe report forms, established an advisory council to
advise the secretary on establishing and monitoring compliance requirements, required administrators to keep records for five years, called for personnel handling these
funds to be fidelity bonded, and made bribery and embezzlement, but not kickbacks, criminal offenses. In addition,
at the insistence of insurance companies, reporting was
limited to plans with one hundred or more participants,
which eliminated some 60 to 70 percent of those previously covered. Although these changes closed some of the
loopholes in the law, other concerns remained uncor-
rected. Disclosure requirements were still inadequate, and

the law did not address serious problems such as determining eligibility, vesting, and termination of welfare and pension plans. Corrupt union officials continued to despoil their pension and welfare funds.[12]

Early in January 1958 President Eisenhower had asked Congress for legislation to implement the rackets committee's interim report recommendations on pension and welfare plans and its suggestions for other union reforms. In his special message he also asked for amendments to the Taft-Hartley Act, including some he had tried unsuccessfully to get in 1953 and 1954. He recommended eliminating the no-man's-land where neither the NLRB nor the states asserted jurisdiction and to permit building trades and construction unions to be established without specific elections. All these were changes Taft had approved before he died. Eisenhower also believed the noncommmunist affidavit was made unnecessary by the Communist Control Act of 1954. He further wanted an amendment providing that parties to a collective bargaining agreement would not be required to renegotiate the contract before its expiration unless the contract provided for such renegotiations, and he wanted authority to appoint an "acting General Counsel" for the NLRB when that office became vacant during a congressional recess. As he had promised when he obtained passage of the Welfare and Pensions Plans Act, Kennedy began hearings on these and other changes in the national labor policy.[13]

Kennedy's subcommittee held thorough hearings and on 10 June 1958 reported S. 3974, the Labor-Management Reporting Act, popularly known as the Kennedy-Ives bill, to the Senate. The measure provided for financial disclosures by unions and for reporting on any attempts to interfere with NLRB rights and with trusteeships. It called for criminal penalties for destroying union records and for union officers to make payments to middlemen. International officers must be elected every five years and local officials every four years, by secret ballot, and candidates could not use union funds to promote their candidacy. It would re-solve the no-man's-land problem as unions wanted it and provided for a new definition of the term *supervisor* to solve the problem of certain craft workers exercising juris-diction over their unskilled fellow workers. It would place a ban on shakedown picketing and improper unloading fees. It provided for prehire arrangements in the building and construction industries with a seven-day union-shop agreement with no required voting by members for choice of agent (this was considered necessary by both employers and employees because the contractor had to be certain of his labor costs before bidding on a contract). It would re-store voting rights to economic strikers, make embezzle-ment a crime, and prohibit individuals convicted of a crime or violation of reporting requirements from holding a union office. Republican members of the committee voted to report the measure but wanted a stronger law and reserved the right to offer amendments during the debate.

In general, the bill was opposed by the NAM, the U.S. Chamber of Commerce, and the UMW, teamsters, and steelworkers unions. It was supported by the AFL-CIO as necessary in its struggle to rid unions of racketeering, but only after George Meany made his often-quoted statement to the Kennedy subcommittee, "God save us from our friends."[14]

According to George Reedy, the bill was written by Ar-thur Goldberg, special counsel for the AFL-CIO, and Archi-bald Cox of the Harvard Law School. He warned Johnson that the proposal departed from the philosophy of the rackets committee report because it was a "disclosure" rather than a "regulatory" measure and said it was ques-tionable whether Senator McClellan would support it. The proposal contained *"absolutely everything* that the AFL-CIO will take without explosion," and if Kennedy were forced to accept significant modifications union leaders would accuse him of bad faith. Reedy told Johnson that the bill was leaked to the press a week before it was to be reported to the Senate and the United Press described it as "one too weak to satisfy Senators who want to correct labor abuses." This story, he was certain, would lend credence to Goldwater's description of the proposal as a "sweetheart bill" that union officials could support.[15]

Two days later Reedy summarized the position of labor leaders in regard to legislation controlling union racketeering. The Democratic party was rightfully considered to be friendly to labor, and unions were certain to gain even more friends in the upcoming elections. But Democrats could not afford to be perceived as being friendly to "labor racketeers," and if unions "wrecked" antiracketeering legislation in the current session "the American people would blame the Democratic party." If union officials tried to block the Kennedy-Ives bill, he warned, they would face not only a Republican Congress in 1959 but one that *feels it has a mandate* to 'crack down' on labor." "Tough" legislation could be written only if the conservative coalition held together, he reasoned, and that coalition could be broken if a sufficient number of northern Democrats supported civil rights legislation desired by liberal Republicans. It was in the best interests of labor leaders to conduct themselves carefully in regard to S. 3974 or they could drive southern Democrats into the arms of northern Republicans, who wanted tough labor legislation.[16]

Secretary of Labor James Mitchell, attending a labor conference of the International Labor Organization in Geneva, issued a statement through the office of the Department of Labor that the administration objected to the Kennedy-Ives bill. He believed it was inadequate to correct the problems disclosed by the rackets committee. It would exempt "more than 60% of labor unions from its provisions," and "paper locals like those controlled by ... Johnny Dio" would be permitted to remain concealed. He declared that it gave the secretary of labor "inadequate powers" to conduct investigations and would not correct the no-man's-land problem. Because of "imperfection, omissions or loopholes" the bill failed to meet President Eisenhower's recommendations of the previous January. If enacted, the proposals "would delude the workers of this country and the American public into believing they had protection they did not in fact have." The Eisenhower administration "decided to press for amendments to bring the bill into line with the President's recommendations." After reading this statement, Reedy concluded that the administration's strategy was "designed to split off the South and appeal to it to 'lynch' labor." John Kennedy was outraged by Mitchell's statement. He told reporters he had just been in contact with "responsible Department of Labor officials," and they had indicated "no opposition whatsoever" to his bill. He felt betrayed.[17]

Senate debate began on the Kennedy-Ives bill on 12 June 1958. In his opening remarks Senator Ives informed his colleagues that "most" of the committee members had been bipartisan in their work, and this was fortunate because "partisan politics has no business in labor-management relations legislation." He paid tribute to his cosponsor by noting that Kennedy's bipartisan attitude had been essential. "Some persons may talk all they want about his being a candidate [for the presidency]," Ives declared, "but I say now that he is about the most bipartisan person I have seen around here." Ives added that he was sorely tempted to sponsor an amendment to his bill to bar discrimination in employment but declined to do so because southerners would then kill the entire bill with a filibuster. This would wreck the bipartisan efforts to pass labor legislation.[18]

Republican senators sponsored a number of administration amendments and other changes, some of which were accepted. These included empowering the secretary of labor to issue subpoenas and requiring him to provide simplified reporting forms for small unions. Union officials had to send their reports to each of their members, and officials who failed to report a conflict of interest could not hold union office. Others removed all exemptions from financial reporting and prohibited a union from hiring any person for a position paying more than $4,000 annually if he failed to file the required reports. Criminal penalties were provided for filing false reports, and felons were barred from holding union office. Finally, a looser definition of a labor organization was added. One administration measure that Goldwater sponsored that would remove the section defining *supervisor* failed to gain approval. But the Arizona senator noted that the other approved amendments corrected all the points that James Mitchell had called for in his press release. In addition, Karl Mundt won approval for his amendments to require that union reports on trusteeships be made available to union members and to extend the noncommunist affidavit to employers.[19]

John Kennedy gained the crucial support of John McClellan for his bill. The only objection the Arkansas senator expressed was to Title VI of the measure, the so-called "sweeteners" union officials wanted to amend the Taft-Hartley Act. McClellan offered an amendment to delete the section on prehires in the building and construction industries, but this lost by a vote of sixty to twenty-nine. The amended bill then passed the Senate eighty-eight to one. Obviously, many senators believed the proposal inadequate to correct union abuses but voted for it as better than nothing.

Secretary of Labor Mitchell described himself as "pleased and heartened" with the Senate amendments to correct "some of the deficiencies and omissions" that he had called to the Senate's attention, and he expressed the hope that the House would make further corrections to comply with the president's requests. The White House staff was apprehensive that if the House passed the Kennedy bill unchanged, President Eisenhower would have to veto it as too "soft" and it would be difficult to explain to the voters why he had vetoed a measure labeled "labor reform."[20]

The House of Representatives received the bill on 18 June. Meanwhile, Republican members of the House Committee on Education and Labor had been endeavoring to report out a proposal that would meet the president's requests of January 1958. When they were unable to force Carl Perkins, Democrat from Kentucky, to call a subcommittee meeting, Republican members appealed to Graham Barden, and he persuaded Perkins to call a meeting on 5 March. At that meeting the subcommittee voted five Democrats to three Republicans not to hold hearings on the president's request for labor legislation. Frustrated here, Robert Griffin, Republican from Michigan, in a meeting of the full committee on 8 May, moved that the subcommittee be discharged and the full committee begin hearings. His motion lost by sixteen Democrats to thirteen Republicans. It was not until 28 May that the subcommittee reluctantly began to hold hearings. As Cleveland Bailey, West Virginia Democrat and member of the full Committee on Education and Labor, noted, there was "a substantial majority" in the House of Representatives who wanted "to enact punitive labor legislation" and the Democrats were determined "to prevent any such catastrophe."[21]

The Democratic majority in the House was determined not to hold extensive hearings and thus prevent Republicans from proposing "punitive legislation" in committee. Speaker Sam Rayburn, Democrat from Texas, sat on the Kennedy-Ives bill for forty days. His official explanation was that he was waiting for the House Committee on Education and Labor to report out the welfare and pension funds bill first and did not want a "mixup." Once the Welfare and Pension Funds Act was safely in conference, he sent the Kennedy-Ives bill to Barden's committee on 29 July. The House Committee on Education and Labor then voted twenty-two to seven against calling up the bill. Two weeks later the committee voted sixteen Democrats to thirteen Republicans not to call up a bill introduced by

Carroll Kearns, Republican from Pennsylvania and member of the Education and Labor Committee, that embodied Eisenhower's requests. Rayburn's strategy was to keep labor legislation bottled up in committee until the closing days of the session in August. Then he would call the Kennedy-Ives bill for consideration with a forty-minute debate and no possibility for amendments under a special House rule that required a two-thirds vote.[22]

On 31 July the Industrial Union Department of the AFL-CIO voted unanimously to telegraph the president, the secretary of labor, and the House leaders, insisting that both the Welfare and Pension Funds bill and the Kennedy-Ives measure be enacted that session. Although many of the amendments the Senate added to the Kennedy-Ives bill were "clearly unwise and unworkable," the telegram noted, and some of them were "clearly unfair and oppressive . . . it still retains enough substantive anti-corruption sections to make it worthwhile." On 16 August, two days before S. 3974 was to be voted on in the House, Democratic Congressmen Lee Metcalf of Montana, George McGovern of South Dakota, Morris Udall of Arizona, Frank Thompson of New Jersey, and James Roosevelt of California circulated a letter in the House of Representatives endorsing the Kennedy-Ives bill. All of these representatives had voted in committee against holding hearings on the bill.[23]

With the time limit on debate on the Kennedy-Ives bill—twenty minutes for each side—not much of substance could be said. Charles Brown, Democrat from Missouri, observed, "Never have I seen such a supercharged, pressurized atmosphere as that surrounding the Kennedy-Ives bill. On all sides there is hate, fear, and retaliation" from pressure groups. Robert Griffin admitted that the measure contained "many sound and constructive provisions" but there were some that were "bad and harmful." The latter included, he believed, applying the noncommunist affidavit to employers, failing to make extortion

truly illegal, and ignoring organizational and minority
picketing problems. He favored Eisenhower's request on
no-man's-land rather than the Kennedy-Ives proposal that
the NLRB assert jurisdiction in this area. Southerners and
Republicans alike wanted the states to assume this jurisdiction because many state laws provided less stringent
protection for union members than did the national policy.
Griffin also opposed the section that required employers to
file reports if they spent over $5,000 to influence their em-
ployees concerning bargaining rights. As George Mc-
Govern noted, this provision had drawn the ire of the
NAM and the national Chamber of Commerce.[24]

The House voted 190 yes to 198 nay to suspend the rules
on the bill, far short of the necessary two-thirds. Of those
voting yes, 149 were Democrats (71 percent of those voting) and 41 were Republicans (23 percent); 61 Democrats
voted no (29 percent) and were joined by 137 Republicans
(77 percent of those voting). George Reedy had earlier predicted to Lyndon Johnson that "it would be almost impossible to get a bill out of the House committee." But once
the Senate acted, the situation would "change overnight"
because any member who would vote to kill the Senate bill
in the House would "voluntarily vote his own retirement."
Evidently the House leaders concurred in this assessment
because of the strategy they followed for winning approval
of the measure, but almost half of the House membership
proved it to be erroneous.[25]

Both parties were determined to make labor reform an
issue in the upcoming elections. Blame and recriminations
flowed from all sides following this vote. Columnist James
Reston was quick to fault the "strange partnership" of the
United States Chamber of Commerce, the National Association of Manufacturers, and the teamsters union. He
called attention to the message the Chamber of Commerce
sent to its members after this House vote that said "your
efforts on behalf of sound labor legislation have been re-
warded." Senator Ives declared that the defeat of the bill

was "an open invitation to all criminals to make the most of their opportunities in the labor-management field." He also noted "an unholy alliance" of major employer groups, the teamsters, the United Mine Workers, and the steel-workers in opposition to the measure. He lamented that la-bor law was going to be an issue in the November elections and that during the debates both sides had been "at great pains to make a record for that issue."[26]

Sam Rayburn blamed the Republican members of the House. He observed that 149 Democrats voted for the bill, but they could not muster enough Republican votes—only 41 out of 201 supported it. John Kennedy concluded that "only Jimmy Hoffa can rejoice at his continued good luck. Honest union members and the general public can only re-gard it as a tragedy that politics" had prevented the Rack-ets Committee recommendations from being enacted. The AFL-CIO blamed Secretary of Labor James Mitchell for op-posing "constructive" reform legislation. Secretary Mitch-ell faulted John Kennedy and the Democrats for not enacting Eisenhower's proposals and quoted Graham Bar-den as saying that "not a single person connected with the leadership of this House requested me to bring the Ken-nedy-Ives bill out." If the House leadership wanted a labor reform law, it was "obvious that as experienced, skillful and talented a leader and parliamentarian as Speaker Sam Rayburn" could have gotten such a bill through the House. Mitchell noted that Rayburn's strategy of calling up the Kennedy-Ives bill by special rule had shocked Barden, and the North Carolinian had declared that it was "the most dangerous and the most far-reaching piece of legislation" in labor-management relations to come to the House "since the Taft-Hartley bill." It was impossible for con-gressmen to understand it and "do the wise thing" in just forty minutes, he complained.[27]

President Eisenhower issued a statement saying he was disappointed that Congress had not passed legislation to "curb the racketeering, corruption, and abuses" revealed by

the McClellan Committee. He reproached Sam Rayburn
for bringing the Kennedy-Ives bill to a vote under procedures that allowed no amendments. On the campaign trail
that fall in California the president declared that his recommendations had been "sidetracked in favor of an insipid
and wholly unsatisfactory substitute." *Newsweek* also
blamed Rayburn, noting that the situation was made to order for Republicans who were "convinced even labor rank
and file wants corrective laws." The news journal noted
that Rayburn's delaying tactics allowed the NAM and
other groups sufficient time to "lobby vigorously" against
the proposal and that "key Republicans" said they would
"rather have the issue than the bill."[28]

At least one person emerged from the situation with an
enhanced reputation. James Reston credited John Kennedy
with undertaking the tough job of getting labor reform legislation through Congress. In the process the senator
fought and won a battle with George Meany. He "took on
and licked" Secretary of Labor James Mitchell. Although
all his efforts "failed to prevail against the massive preju-
dices of several powerful groups" in the House of Representatives, Kennedy had successfully piloted his measure
through the Senate. In the process of doing so, Reston
wrote, the young senator from Massachusetts won the
unanimous respect of his colleagues. The Kennedy name
(many people confused John with Robert or thought they
were one and the same in connection with the rackets
committee and labor reform legislation) was now closely
associated with labor law, and John Kennedy could campaign on this issue for reelection in November 1958. When
he returned to the Senate, his name on a labor law would
enhance his chances for running for president.[29]

Meanwhile, congressmen and senators were gearing up
for the fall campaigns. In the midst of debate on the Kennedy-Ives bill, George Reedy sent Lyndon Johnson a confidential memo suggesting that he "try this out on some of
your conservative friends." The U.S. Chamber of Com-

merce and the National Association of Manufacturers were working on the assumption that if they could block the Kennedy-Ives measure, they would be able to get a "strong" labor bill in 1959. If Kennedy-Ives were enacted in 1958, Reedy reasoned, there probably would not be "any more labor legislation for a number of years." But conservatives needed a lesson in "some elementary arithmetic." The newly admitted state of Alaska would elect two senators that were certain to be prolabor, and thirty-four other Senate seats were at stake that year. Knowland was going to run for governor of California on his record of fighting for strong labor legislation, and Edward Martin of Pennsylvania was resigning. These two antilabor senators would be replaced by prolabor men *no matter what happens.* Either Clare Engle or Goodwin Knight would be elected in California and either George Leader or Hugh Scott in Pennsylvania would win. Reedy believed that in the case of eleven other seats a switch from antilabor to prolabor was "better than even" and for two—from Tennessee and from Wisconsin—the antilabor odds were "less than even." He concluded that in 1959 in voting on tough labor legislation, the division would be sixty to thirty-eight "on the side of labor." This thirty-eight included conceding all of the deep South seats to conservatives, except for Lister Hill and John Sparkman of Alabama, Olin D. Johnston of South Carolina, and Estes Kefauver of Tennessee. Reedy then asked whether conservatives really wanted to wait until 1959 for the Senate to write a new labor bill, or whether they would not be better advised to support the Kennedy-Ives proposal as better than nothing.[30]

The recession of 1957, which had not yet run its course, played a part in the elections of 1958 in a number of states. By February 1958 unemployment, holding at about 7 percent nationally, was particularly acute in some places and the Eisenhower administration labeled 118 areas in twenty-six states "distressed areas." By April unemployment reached 7.7 percent, the highest since 1941, and

Democrats in Congress began pressing for a large increase in public works. The Democratic-controlled Congress established the Area Redevelopment Administration, but the president vetoed it in September. In July the economy began an upturn, but by November some areas were still severely depressed economically, which helped the candidacy of a number of Democrats, who emphasized the reluctance of Republicans to assist the economy directly.[31]

Organized labor was particularly interested in two of the senatorial races. William Knowland, Senate minority leader, had presidential aspirations. His strategy to reach the White House was not to run for reelection to the Senate but for governor of California against Attorney General Edmond "Pat" Brown. He would have to eliminate Goodwin Knight from that race, forcing Knight to run as the Republican candidate for Knowland's Senate seat, which upset Knight and many of his supporters. Knowland based his campaign on all-out support for the right-to-work law that was before the California voters, a "path to political suicide," as one writer put it, and to demand stronger labor legislation that would clean up unions. As a result, organized labor staged a huge effort to get hundreds of thousands of Democrats registered in that predominantly Democratic state, spending, according to Republican estimates, anywhere from $5 million to $25 million. "Nowhere in the nation," Newsweek reported, "did organized labor fight so hard, or spend so much money," and Knowland's positions on labor issues "foreordained his own defeat." Knight lost badly, as did Knowland, and the former angrily attributed his defeat to the right-to-work proposition, noting that Californians had defeated the proposal previously and it was a mistake for Knowland to make it an issue again.[32]

In Arizona the handsome, personable Barry Goldwater, president of Goldwater Department Store in Phoenix, had received his political baptism in campaigning successfully for a state right-to-work law in the late 1940s. He was swept into the Senate by the Eisenhower landslide of 1952 and quickly won the animosity of labor leaders with his antiunion attitude. Labor staged a major effort to defeat him in 1958. But Goldwater's home city contained half of the state's population and Eugene C. Pulliam, editor of the *Phoenix Gazette* and the *Arizona Republic*, the state's largest newspapers, hated "taxes and labor unions." Pulliam's newspapers diligently reported late in the campaign that Goldwater's mother had been receiving numerous telephone calls reminding her of the fate of Victor Reisel, the labor news reporter who had been blinded by acid thrown in his face following his stories about corruption in unions. In the last two days of the campaign, leaflets were circulated about a "diabolical plot" in Arizona. The leaflets claimed that Goldwater's election would "help Stalin's plan" because the mine, mill and smelter workers, a communist-infiltrated union, had endorsed him. Goldwater won easily, but many Arizonans who voted for him split their ticket and voted for Stewart Udall for Congress, a Democrat who was endorsed by the AFL-CIO Committee on Political Education (COPE).[33]

Walter Reuther confessed that he was the "phantom candidate" in more than twenty states for governor, U.S. senator, and assorted congressional seats. To stress the labor issue, the staff of the Republican Policy Committee issued a monograph entitled *The Labor Bosses: America's Third Party*. It emphasized that "the hold of the labor bosses on the Democratic Party has, for all practical purposes, rendered responsible Democratic leadership virtually impotent." This angered the Democratic national chairman, who responded that "practically all of the labor leaders" the McClellan Committee had found to be corrupt were supporters of Republican candidates for office. Also, in Indiana Democrats stressed that the carpenters president, Maurice Hutcheson, long a Republican supporter, had been indicted in a state highway scandal.[34]

Republican Hugh Scott won his race in depression-ridden Pennsylvania because of a splintering of Democrats there, but the recession aided Democrat Vance Hartke in

his victory in Indiana, and Philip Hart in Michigan swept
Republican Charles Potter from the Senate, at least in part
because the recession had hit hard in the automobile state.
Antilabor Senators William Jenner of Indiana and H. Alexander Smith of New Jersey retired and John Bricker lost in
Ohio, so George Reedy's predictions were realized in the
next Congress. It was strongly prolabor. John Kennedy believed he needed a majority of 500,000 in his race to give
credibility to his presidential aspirations. His majority was
874,608, the largest ever won by a candidate in Massachusetts and the biggest majority of any senatorial candidate
in 1958. In the new House of Representatives, Democrats
more than doubled their margin of control. The Eighty-
fifth Congress had 235 Democrats and 200 Republicans;
the Eighty-sixth Congress was composed of 281 Democrats
and 153 Republicans. The Senate changed from 50 Democrats and 46 Republicans to 64 Democrats and 34 Republicans. This was the largest Democratic majority in
Congress since 1937. Right-to-work laws lost in California,
Colorado, Idaho, Ohio, and Washington and won only in
Kansas by 76,500 votes. Seventy percent of the candidates
supported by unions were elected. Postmaster General
Arthur Summerfield warned that the United States now
"teeters on the precipice of a labor-bossed Congress."
Newsweek noted that Eisenhower had angered labor leaders in 1958 when he promised to "fumigate" the labor
movement and that the first test of his lame-duck role
would come when he sent a new labor reform bill to Congress in January. Republicans had made labor leaders mad
in California and Ohio, the magazine stated, and the party
now needed to convince unions that it was not an antiunion party but one "merely of reform."[35]

President Eisenhower had lost Sherman Adams, his
chief of staff, and his resignation became a political issue
in the 1958 elections. In February 1958 the House Committee on Legislative Oversight began investigating the relationship between Adams and Bernard Goldfine, a

wealthy New England industrialist. The two had been friends for years, and whenever Goldfine had problems with the Federal Trade Commission or the Securities Exchange Commission he naturally called on his friend for assistance. It was revealed that Adams had received an expensive Oriental rug and a vicuna coat from the textiler and that Goldfine had paid some of Adams's hotel bills when he visited New England. Adams admitted he had made a mistake in accepting the coat and said that the rug was a loan and he saw nothing wrong in staying in his friend's hotel room when he was in Boston. He had not sought special favors for anyone but had merely done the routine thing in official Washington by making telephone calls of inquiry for Goldfine. The committee cleared him of wrongdoing after he admitted he had been indiscreet.

As the Adams-Goldfine investigation dragged on and the elections approached, nervous Republicans began to demand that Adams be fired. "I need him," Eisenhower plaintively replied, but when Edmund Muskie and the Democrats swept Maine in its September elections, leading Republicans demanded Adams's scalp and Eisenhower had to yield. He sent Gerald Morgan, deputy assistant to the president, to deliver the news. Wilton B. "Jerry" Persons replaced Adams as assistant to the president, and the change was soon apparent. Adams had been the cool, hardnosed New Englander who never took time to say hello or goodbye on the telephone. Persons, by contrast, according to *Time* magazine, operated on the theory that "the way to lead Congress is to exploit the natural desire to work and plan for common ends." This new approach would be effective in getting a labor reform law in 1959.[36]

Finally, the elections of 1958 brought a change in Republican congressional leadership. Twice previously Charles Halleck of Indiana had sought to displace Joseph Martin of Massachusetts as minority leader in the House. Both times he failed for lack of support from Eisenhower because the president did not want to risk splitting his party. Following the election, in December 1958 fourteen Republican congressmen met in the office of Robert Wilson of California to discuss the House leadership situation. They ranged from Wisconsin right-winger John Byrnes to Michigan's middle-roader Gerald Ford. They concluded that the Republican party had met with disaster in the elections because of "inept Republican House leadership." Specifically, they cited Martin for not keeping them informed of House business, for losing touch so he could no longer represent Republican congressional thinking to the White House, and for rarely calling a session of the House Policy Committee. They told Halleck they would support him if he would promise to address these problems.[37]

Halleck was by nature a conservative but during his years in Congress had swallowed his Tory instincts, "voting with the center of his party," and had served his party well as a leader in the House of Representatives. His "middleman characteristics," David Truman noted, fit the requirements of a floor leader. He played golf at Burning Tree with Eisenhower more often than anyone else on Capitol Hill and had become a spokesman for the middle-of-the-road Eisenhower administration. With this encouragement from his colleagues, Halleck asked Gerald Morgan to sound out the president on his candidacy. This time Eisenhower gave his approval, and Halleck defeated Martin for the minority leadership by four votes. Knowland's race for the California governorship left his position in the Senate open. Conservative Republican senators were able to elect Everett McKinley Dirksen of Illinois as their leader. In the next few years the "Ev and Charlie Show" gained widespread national notoriety as these two natural showmen took to the air periodically to present the Republican program to the people via television.[38]

Labor leaders could, and did, interpret the elections of 1958 as a major victory. They were confident the Eighty-sixth Congress would be strongly prolabor and that there was no possibility of its passing punitive legislation.

5. Senator Kennedy Tries Again

The McClellan Rackets Committee issued its interim report in March 1958 but continued its investigations through 1959. Its revelations of corruption in labor-management relations fueled an ever-increasing public demand for reform. A Gallup poll conducted 7 to 12 November 1958 asked what legislation the new Congress should pass. The school integration crisis ranked first; second was the desire to "clean up corruption and racketeering in unions." A poll conducted during the second week in January 1959 showed that only 6 percent of the respondents regarded labor laws as "too strict," while 49 percent believed they were "not strict enough," 20 percent "about right," and 25 percent had no opinion.[1]

Union leaders had reason to be confident that they would not face tough legislation because of the elections of 1958. Some thirty congressmen who had voted against the Kennedy bill did not return to the Eighty-sixth Congress. When it convened, the Democrats added four liberals to the House Subcommittee on Education and Labor to make it as "safe for labor" as the Senate Subcommittee on Labor and Public Welfare. But the Republicans put two ultra-right-wingers on the subcommittee so it still contained a majority of southern Democrats and "GOP Tories." Union leaders, though, placed their trust in John Kennedy's Senate Subcommittee on Labor and Public Welfare. The AFL-CIO's COPE evaluated the voting record of the senators who

served on the subcommittee on previous legislation that
was important to labor. The results were as follows:

Democrats		*Republicans*	
John Kennedy	15-0	Barry Goldwater	0-13
Pat McNamara	16-0	Everett Dirksen	5-11
Wayne Morse	15-1		

Jennings Randolph, Democrat from West Virginia, and
Winston Prouty, Vermont Republican, were new to the
committee. Randolph would vote prolabor and Prouty antilabor. Other Democrats who would play important parts in
labor legislation in 1959 were rated thus by COPE:

John McClellan	7-7
Lyndon Johnson	13-3
Hubert Humphrey	14-0
Paul Douglas	16-0[2]

The labor issues of 1958 remained the same the next
year. There was a public demand for reform legislation.
Management groups were strongly united in their opposition to changes in Taft-Hartley desired by labor officials
but did want to amend the law to make all secondary boycotts and hot cargo agreements illegal and to ban organizational picketing. Unions, however, were badly divided.
Although few affiliates in the AFL-CIO opposed reform
legislation, most wanted the NLRB to assert jurisdiction
in the no-man's-land area and to amend Taft-Hartley to
allow economic strikers to vote in representational elections. The maritime and building and construction
unions wished to legalize prehire agreements, and the latter wanted to legalize common situs picketing, a union
weapon that prevented work by all workers on a single
construction site involved in a labor dispute. The communications union desired a new definition of the term *super-*

visor. These changes were known as Taft-Hartley sweeteners, to "sweeten" a labor reform bill so that unions would support it.

Based on the experience of 1958, the Democratic leadership in 1959 decided on a "two-package" approach. John Kennedy announced that he would first get a labor reform bill through the Senate and would then work on a separate bill that would embody changes in Taft-Hartley. On 6 February 1959 the Senate approved Kennedy's request for $20,000 to establish a special panel of labor experts to study needed changes in the Taft-Hartley Act. The "blue ribbon panel," chaired by Archibald Cox, included David Cole, Guy Farmer, Arthur Goldberg, Charles Gregory, Clark Kerr, Denison Kitchel, Plato Papps, Gerard Reilly, Louis Sherman, Russell Smith, and Willard Wirtz. The committee was instructed to make its recommendations by 1 June 1959. Unfortunately, Clark Kerr was the only economist in the group; the others were lawyers. The panel adjourned for the summer without reporting and reconvened that fall. It issued a report in February 1960, after the labor reform bill was already enacted, recommending a complete reorganization of the NLRB and abolishing the office of general counsel. Thus Kennedy's panel of "experts" had no official impact on labor legislation in 1959.

Kennedy soon discovered that some labor leaders would not support labor reform legislation without some sweeteners. They argued that the Eisenhower administration supported some of the desired changes, and they had enjoyed great success in the elections of 1958; therefore, they should not settle for less than what had been proposed in the Kennedy bill the previous year. The executive council of the AFL-CIO met in San Juan, Puerto Rico, in February 1959 and developed its strategy of insisting on Taft-Hartley sweeteners as the price for supporting reform legislation. Senator Kennedy was forced to accept this decision and again introduced the bill that had been defeated in the House of Representatives in 1958.[3]

Kennedy's bill again was too mild for the Eisenhower administration. Secretary of Labor James Mitchell sent the president the results of a Department of Labor study of newspaper editorials concerning labor reform. Thirty-four of the fifty-seven editorials supported the administration's position, three favored Kennedy's bill, and twenty discussed alternatives without indicating strong preference.[4] A month before he received this survey, Eisenhower sent a special message to Congress outlining his views on labor reform legislation.

Eisenhower called for a twenty-point program, many items of which he had been requesting since his first year in office. Specifically, he wanted to require annual financial reports to be filed with the Department of Labor and with union membership, proper records on all items that had to be reported, records of all payments, investments, and financial transactions, and criminal penalties for bribery, embezzlement, or destruction of records. He asked that union constitutions and by-laws establishing secret ballots to elect officers be made public, that provision be made for periodic secret elections, and that it be illegal to use union funds for campaigning for office. Unions should be forced to administer funds for the benefit of their members and provision should be made for the rank and file to sue their unions for misconduct. He asked for greater control over the use of trusteeships that were established for corrupt or undemocratic affiliates. He wanted to preserve all current remedies under state and national laws. He again called for permitting secondary boycotts on all struck work that was farmed out, forbidding jurisdictional picketing, and giving states jurisdiction over no-man's-land cases. He wanted to give the NLRB discretionary power to determine voting by economic strikers, to allow the NLRB to certify building and construction unions without elections, and to permit the board to hold representational elections without prior hearings. As he had urged for several years, the noncommunist affidavit should be extended to employers, and the renegotiation of contracts during their lifetimes should be forbidden unless the contract had a provision for reopening negotiations. Finally, he added three new requests: to permit the president to name an interim general counsel for the NLRB, to require that no more than three NLRB members be from the same political party, and to empower the secretary of labor to administer the law.[5]

Although both the Eisenhower and Kennedy proposals called for secret elections and financial reporting, in response to the McClellan Committee revelations, the president's other requests were much less palatable to union officials than the Kennedy bill. Eisenhower called for more drastic penalties on union racketeering, more severe restrictions on extortion picketing, and more curbs on secondary boycotts. More important, Kennedy wanted to follow the two-proposal approach and make changes in Taft-Hartley after enactment of labor reform legislation. Administration strategists decided that because of the McClellan Committee hearings, reform legislation was mandatory. Significant labor legislation seldom emerged from Congress, however, and, therefore, reform legislation and Taft-Hartley changes must be put together in one package. It would take a miracle for this lame-duck president to get his labor program out of Congress because, as his congressional liaison for labor legislation described it, the administration's operating slogan on tough legislation in 1959-60 was, "do we have one-third plus one in Congress?" The Democrats had overwhelming control of the Eighty-sixth Congress so the most the administration could realistically expect was to persuade Congress to sustain a veto. In his last two years in office Eisenhower used the veto twenty-three times and was overridden only once, thanks to the conservative coalition.[6]

Management spokesmen, of course, supported the administration both in approach and in topics to be covered in labor reform legislation. In their view, enactment of

Taft-Hartley sweeteners in a reform bill would lessen the possibility that unions might compromise later on changes in Taft-Hartley desired by management. When Kennedy's Subcommittee on Labor and Public Welfare held hearings on his bill, S. 505, the first management witness to appear stated this position. Management was "against the inclusion of nonrelevant Taft-Hartley amendments in a measure like S. 505, which is primarily a corruption proposal, unless all needed Taft-Hartley amendments are included at this time." If changes were to be made in the Taft-Hartley Act, secondary boycotts and jurisdictional picketing should be curbed.[7]

Labor unions, of course, had participated in the writing of the Kennedy-Ervin bill (when Senator Ives retired in 1958, Kennedy persuaded Sam Ervin to cosponsor his bill). During the hearings Kennedy openly courted AFL-CIO suggestions for changes in the language of his proposal, and the only significant union testimony came from Andrew Biemiller, the official spokesman for the AFL-CIO, who said that unions would oppose any reform legislation that did not include Taft-Hartley sweeteners.[8]

When Secretary of Labor Mitchell testified, Kennedy was ready for him. By this time the senator had become an expert in labor law. He was joined by Senator Morse, former dean of the University of Oregon School of Law and an expert in labor legislation, and the two were prepared with a series of questions about hypothetical situations. Neither Mitchell nor the solicitor general for the Department of Labor, Stuart Rothman, was expecting this onslaught, and they had to admit frequently that they did not know the applicability of the administration's proposals to unfavorable situations or that the result of their ideas sometimes would be embarrassingly negative. When Kennedy attacked the administration bill because it would prohibit picketing of sweatshops operating under "sweetheart" contracts and would punish honest locals for dishonest behavior of their national officers by denying them NLRB services, Rothman was forced to admit, "You may be correct, senator." Reporters particularly enjoyed this exchange because Kennedy was being mentioned frequently as a presidential candidate and Mitchell was being touted as a possible Republican candidate for the vice-presidency. Mitchell, a Roman Catholic from New Jersey, would bring balance to the ticket with Nixon and also was one of the few Republicans who could help draw the labor vote away from the Democrats.[9] But Kennedy did not press political issues here and concluded the interchange with a call for bipartisan legislation.

Senate Majority Leader Lyndon Johnson, who would play a crucial role in any forthcoming labor legislation, was also frequently mentioned as a potential Democratic presidential nominee. George Reedy, his legislative aide and an expert in labor law, reported that labor law was the one area of legislation Johnson did not understand so "he left all these labor matters entirely" for Reedy to decide and to explain to him. The majority leader "had literally no understanding" of how unions operated, and he "got into an awful lot of trouble over and over again." Reedy found this to be "rather peculiar" because labor leaders liked Johnson. "Walter Reuther really liked him" and so did George Meany. Reedy wrote him a lengthy memo suggesting a political strategy for the coming year. Reedy listed among the liabilities of being "in the Presidential picture" that it would make Johnson "the target of envious candidates" and intensify "the opposition of ultra liberals . . . who feel you are frustrating them." Yet there were assets to the situation. As long as Texans considered him a presidential possibility, "significant Texas opposition to you is unlikely," uncommitted Democrats would refrain from attacking him, and "able men will be drawn to you who, if handled carefully, can be helpful in many ways." Based on this analysis, Reedy recommended that Johnson continue to declare that he was not a candidate, to "disconcert the party professionals at well-planned intervals by accepting speaking engagements in Northern states where your appearance has not been anticipated," and to encourage the current impression that he could not be nominated because the party professionals "are bending to the pressure groups."[10]

During the subcommittee hearings on the Kennedy-Ervin bill, Johnson was under considerable pressure to get Title VI, the Taft-Hartley sweeteners, deleted but labor officials proved adamant on this issue. Reedy reported two obstacles Johnson faced: "(a) the fact that George Meany is a member of the Building Trades which stand to gain the most from Title VI; (b) The fact that Meany feels he has some understanding with Senator Kennedy." Reedy thought Meany was correct in his interest in getting the prehire provisions because a strict enforcement of the Taft-Hartley ban on the closed shop "would put an end to most craft unions." Since 1947 the building and construction unions had been "bootlegging" these contracts "and will continue to do so." But Meany did not understand Johnson's political problem. Johnson could not "afford to have a Democratic Congress pass a truly anti-labor bill," and Reedy was convinced that that would happen if Title VI remained in the bill. The Taft-Hartley sweeteners opened up the entire field of labor-management relations, and *"if any aspect of labor-management relations is opened up, it will be difficult to prevent all aspects from being opened up."* If that happened in the House, Reedy advised, "labor will come out on the short end of the stick." He concluded with the observation that the strategy Johnson had improvised that morning was correct: "Meany must be made to see the realities of the House situation."[11] But when the subcommittee concluded its hearings, Title VI was still in the bill.

Lyndon Johnson then suggested to Everett Dirksen, a member of both the Subcommittee on Labor and the full Committee on Labor and Public Welfare, that it might be advisable for the Senate to delay its labor bill until the

House had acted on its measure. Dirksen happily agreed. John Kennedy was a front-running candidate for the presidency, and Republicans wanted a stronger law than the Kennedy bill. If Republicans could "knock him down on his pet issue, maybe even keep his name off this major piece of legislation, they could undercut his Presidential chances considerably." At a meeting with Republican legislative leaders, which Eisenhower held almost weekly while Congress was in session, it was "agreed it would be preferable for the House to act before the Senate" on labor reform legislation. Thus, at the first Senate committee meeting, Dirksen moved that the Senate delay action until the House had passed its labor bill. The committee defeated his motion. Senator Goldwater moved that the administration's bill be substituted. Senator Morse moved that the committee report S. 505 directly to the Senate without further discussion. The Democratic majority also defeated these motions.[12]

Following the defeat of Goldwater's motion, the secretary of labor sent the Arizona senator a series of amendments that were based on the administration bill. They were redrafted "with such adjustments as would be necessary to tie them in" with the Kennedy-Ervin bill. Goldwater then introduced about one hundred amendments in committee sessions, most of which were rejected. None of the reforms Eisenhower sought were added to the measure. The committee included some fifty minor amendments in the proposal, but none of them changed the substance of Kennedy's bill, although he made some concessions on language and minor points to gain the support of liberal Republicans. As a result, when the bill was reported to the Senate, it had gained the support of two Republican senators and was labeled the Kennedy-Ervin-Javits-Cooper bill. The full Committee on Labor and Public Welfare voted thirteen to two, Dirksen and Goldwater dissenting, to report S. 505 to the Senate as amended on 25 March 1959. Kennedy then introduced on 14 April what is called a "clean" bill in place of the amended version. It was treated technically as a new measure and was numbered S. 1555.[13]

Senate Report 187 accompanied S. 1555. It noted that the bill would carry out four of the five recommendations of the rackets committee interim report; the fifth one supposedly had been resolved by the Welfare and Pension Plan Disclosure Act of 1958. Disregarding the Title VI sweeteners, the report justified the "two-bills" approach by pointing out that the Committee on Labor and Public Welfare had appointed a panel of experts to advise on other changes needed in the labor-management relations laws (but it did not say the panel had not yet made its report). In doing its work, the committee had followed three basic principles: first, it is desirable to have minimum government interference "in the internal affairs of any organization"; second, as long as democratic safeguards are provided, rank-and-file members are competent to regulate union affairs; and third, remedies for abuses should be direct and thus sanctions should be applied to union officials, not unions. In addition to the Taft-Hartley sweeteners, Title VI included Eisenhower's recommendations for an acting general counsel, extended the noncommunist affidavit to employers, and empowered the secretary of labor to regulate, investigate, and prosecute by obtaining injunctions and other weapons, although he would not have as much authority as the president had proposed.[14]

The minority members (Dirksen and Goldwater) declared that the bill had "weaknesses" and was filled with "gimmicks." It would permit embezzlement to continue, and its provisions on financial reporting, extortion, and picketing were very weak. They believed it would be a good proposal if the Senate would delete the Taft-Hartley amendments; impose fiduciary obligations on union officials; deny tax immunity and access to NLRB services for violators of the law; give no-man's-land jurisdiction to the states; limit minority picketing; close loopholes in the

Taft-Hartley ban on secondary boycotts; and limit union political expenditures and contributions. Republican co-sponsors John Sherman Cooper, from Kentucky, and Jacob Javits, from New York, believed that although the bill was not completely satisfactory to anyone, "it is a wholesome and substantial contribution to the law at this time which is practical and represents material progress." The remaining Republican member, Winston L. Prouty of Vermont, made the point that S. 505 had been improved by Republican amendments in the subcommittee and he hoped the Senate would make further improvements by amending S. 1555.[15]

During the debates, Senate Republicans had the able assistance of Edward A. McCabe, Eisenhower's legislative liaison, who brought them the support and expertise of the White House. McCabe usually served as White House liaison with the Senate, but several years before he had acted as counsel to the House Committee on Education and Labor and was highly regarded by its chairman, Graham Barden. Thus McCabe was given responsibility for developing labor legislation in both houses and played a key role in producing the Landrum-Griffin Act. Gerald Morgan, who played an important part in drafting the Hartley bill in 1947, was deputy assistant to the president and McCabe's immediate superior and also was influential in the struggle for labor reform.

McCabe informed the White House staff that Kennedy's bill was "a very weak gesture . . . and was largely written by the unions." It contained "none of the real reforms recommended by the President," which gave the White House an opportunity to capitalize on its "deficiencies." He noted that, at that late date, there was no possibility, if there ever had been, of getting two bills through Congress that session. He urged that every effort be made to convince Congress that the new law "should cover all major areas of labor racketeering." The average congressman could understand the argument that "it makes no sense to pass laws aimed at union elections and union financing (important though those are) if we indefinitely postpone the laws we need to meet the real racket head on." He noted that this approach would be consistent with the interests of business groups who were insisting on an end to blackmail picketing and secondary boycotts. "True, some of them don't buy all of our program," he noted, "nor we theirs." But the administration should seek "their help in forcing Congress to tackle the whole job. If we can get that done, we can take care of details. If we don't get it done, we all lose." As it turned out, this administration strategy was unsuccessful in the Senate.[16]

As the Senate opened debate on S. 1555, McClellan and Ervin worked behind the scenes to convince Kennedy to return to his two-package approach and eliminate the Title VI sweeteners. If Kennedy would agree to this, they would lend strong support to his reform bill and later would support a bill to amend Taft-Hartley, including the AFL-CIO sweeteners. With Kennedy's cooperation, they would try to prevent the addition of any amendments to the reform measure that unions opposed; if Kennedy did not agree, McClellan would feel free to withdraw his pledge of support and Ervin would withdraw his cosponsorship. Labor leaders, however, again refused to accept this two-package deal, and Kennedy was forced to reject their offer.

Numerous amendments were immediately introduced when the Senate began debate. Goldwater proposed more than seventy and McClellan alone introduced half that many. Soon the senators' desks were stacked with over one hundred long, complicated amendments to be digested and decided on. Sam Ervin's amendment to delete Title VI was the first to be debated.

McClellan supported the North Carolinian in his argument that only the provisions for economic strikers and prehire agreements were in the original bill; the remainder had been added in committee, and they should all be removed from a labor reform measure and acted upon separately. Kennedy responded by citing approvingly a *New York Times* editorial declaring that the defeat of Title VI "would set labor back on its heels in the present session of Congress." The amendment was defeated sixty-seven to twenty-seven, giving Kennedy the first victory.[17]

The following day Dirksen presented an amendment to substitute the administration's bill, which lost sixty-seven to twenty-four. Then McClellan, who believed he had been relieved of his gentleman's obligation to support the Kennedy bill, rose to speak on a series of amendments he wanted to propose. Because of the revelations of his committee hearings, the Arkansas senator had acquired enormous prestige in the field of labor-management relations. He was joined by Ervin, who asked him leading questions, and the two senators delivered a two-hour symposium on the need for labor reform. McClellan then introduced his first amendment. It would insert a new Title I called "Bill of Rights of Members of Labor Organizations." Kennedy immediately spoke in opposition to the amendment, declaring that it was not only unnecessary but deleterious because it would deny more extensive rights available under state laws by preempting the field for federal jurisdiction. McClellan then proposed an amendment to his amendment to preclude that possibility.

John Carroll, Democrat from Colorado, warned his colleagues about a feature of the bill of rights that became a crucial issue later. He noted that the proposal would empower the secretary of labor and the attorney general to seek injunctions to restrain violations of the rights of individuals. He pointed out that this issue had been hotly debated and rejected two years earlier, when the Civil Rights Act of 1957 was enacted. Apparently the southern senators did not pick up on this argument because of the favorable emotion evoked by the term *bill of rights*. Opponents of McClellan's amendment were in an awkward position because he labeled it a bill of rights and they could hardly oppose such a concept, especially when it was presented by

the nation's premier authority on labor-management corruption. The problem was that no one had had an opportunity to read the exact language of his amendment. The
senators had to try, like Kennedy, to find technicalities in
the proposal to defeat it. Kennedy concluded his argument
by again calling attention, as Carroll had, to the injunctive
powers to be authorized for obtaining civil rights and insisted that the amendment was "badly drawn" and, if it
was accepted, union members would have fewer, not more,
rights: "McClellan gave an eloquent summary, asking
Why is it wrong to obtain an injunction to protect the
rights of such workers? Why is it wrong to give the Secretary the right to bring suit to secure an injunction to enforce the rules he makes? I say that union members have
rights; and tonight we shall either protect them by legislative means, or Senators will vote against every dues-paying
member in the country who tonight is being exploited and
abused." A reporter described McClellan's appeal: "At
times he reached crescendoes of oratory that all but cut off
his own breath and voice." His colleagues were obviously
moved by his emotion.[18]

When the roll was called several liberal Republican
senators passed, waiting to see how the vote went. Some
Republicans obviously saw this as an opportunity to vote
against Kennedy. When the vote was completed, the bill of
rights had passed the Senate by vote of forty-seven to forty-
six. Union representatives had been so certain that there
were more than enough votes to prevent the Kennedy bill
from being amended in any significant way that they had
allowed Hubert Humphrey to go to the West Coast to deliver some speeches, and agreed that Paul Douglas could go
to Canada to meet with the prime minister about the
water level of Lake Michigan. In addition to these crucial
votes, Theodore Green, Democrat from Rhode Island, and
A. Willis Robertson, Democrat from West Virginia, were
absent because of illness. Certainly it was a tactical mistake, based on supreme confidence, to allow Humphrey

and Douglas to leave town while the labor bill was being debated. Yet Republicans closed ranks on the issue, and only Jacob Javits and William Langer, Republican from North Dakota, voted against the addition, while several southerners soon discovered that they had voted to extend federal power to protect the rights of individuals.

The Senate made its action final when Goldwater moved to table a motion to reconsider. Before it came to a vote, James Murray, Democrat from Montana, went home, and James Eastland, Democrat from Mississippi, and Everett Jordan, Democrat from North Carolina, were in the Senate cloakroom. Their absence allowed a tie vote, forty-five to forty-five, and Vice-President Nixon cast the deciding vote to table. Many Washington insiders credited Lyndon Johnson, the master vote-counter, with having the two southerners remain in the cloakroom so Nixon would have to commit himself on the issue. Alan McAdams notes that "it is unlikely that these seasoned legislators were unaware of the impact of their absence."[19]

Newsweek saw another Johnson plot in the Senate action on the bill of rights. Two Democrats, Thomas Dodd of Connecticut and Dennis Chavez of New Mexico, voted with McClellan. Both were known as "Johnson men," whom the majority leader called on "when he badly needs votes." The news journal concluded that Johnson had rigged this vote to embarrass his rival for the Democratic presidential nomination, John Kennedy. Johnson's legislative aide, George Reedy, refutes this allegation, saying that in regard to Senate maneuvering, "Johnson would never embarrass another Senator unless there was a very potent reason for doing so. Don't forget," he noted, "the entire Johnson operation was based upon the very firm realization that somewhere he might need somebody's vote." Reedy insisted that he never knew of an instance when Johnson, the master politician, conducted himself so "as to completely preclude getting somebody's vote down the road."[20]

The bill of rights added a huge area in which the national government would control union internal affairs. The amendment gave a very broad definition of a union "member" or "member in good standing" as including "any person who has fulfilled or tendered the lawful requirements for membership in such organization, and who neither has voluntarily withdrawn from membership nor has been expelled or suspended from membership after appropriate proceedings consistent with lawful provisions of the constitution, or bylaws, or other governing charter of such organization." Clearly this definition would be unacceptable to many people, including union leaders and southerners, when they realized its implications. It would, among other things, make it more difficult for honest union leaders to eliminate corruption, it would threaten union officials with punishment for erroneous rulings or procedures, and it would make it possible for undesirables, communists, and Negroes to become members (an anathema to southerners) and have many "rights."

Obviously, the Democratic leadership had to do something about the language in Title I. As the bill of rights was being debated, Archibald Cox (on the floor by Senate permission to provide legal advice) was heard to mutter, "poor draftsmanship." The lawyer who wrote the amendment for McClellan, Monroe Freedman, a former Cox student, later said that even with a biased interpretation, the bill of rights would not have an adverse effect on unions. In any case, labor representatives insisted that Johnson do something, focusing their objections on the loose wording and the definition of members' rights.[21]

Meanwhile, southerners were having second thoughts about voting for the bill of rights. One magazine reported that southern Democrats Richard Russell and Herman Talmadge of Georgia, J. Strom Thurmond of South Carolina, and Harry Byrd of Virginia were "fit to be tied" when they discovered the implications of the proposal they had supported. The bill of rights would involve the national government in the affairs of individuals in the same way as civil rights laws. Senate Majority Leader Johnson received a memorandum from an aide warning that "if this amendment becomes law, it may alter the entire course of civil rights legislation in this Congress" and decided he had to do something. But first he had to solve the problem created by the Senate's vote to table the motion to reconsider. He found a parliamentary tactic that could be used to remove or amend the section by striking out contiguous material and getting around the tabled motion. The next morning he circulated, through the office of Olin Johnston, South Carolina Democrat, a "folksy" memorandum calling attention to the civil rights issue "in emotional and exaggerated terms." He and Kennedy finally decided to modify the section to make it acceptable, probably because they lacked the votes to tear it out of the bill. Archibald Cox then began consulting AFL-CIO lawyers and drafting revisions to remove weaknesses and clarify language.[22]

Meanwhile, other amendments were being considered. Acceptance of the bill of rights opened the possibility of other changes, but it also alerted Kennedy, Johnson, and the AFL-CIO that they could not be overconfident. Some thirty changes were added, most of them minor. Senator Prouty sponsored the most important one, and on 24 April it carried by a vote of eighty-six to four. This amendment would allow organizational picketing unless another union was recognized or the union had lost an NLRB representational election in the previous nine months. But the mood of the Senate was quite different from 1958, when labor had received overwhelming support. This change of attitude was a reflection of the public's changing perception of union bosses. McClellan's amendment to bar secondary boycotts, for example, a proposal that lost by a substantial majority in 1958, lost in 1959 by only five votes, fifty to forty-one.[23]

Several versions of the revised bill of rights soon began to circulate among senators. AFL-CIO lawyers drafted one,

and Frank Church, Democrat from Idaho, and Joseph
Clark, Democrat from Pennsylvania, wrote another one after, some claimed, they had several cocktails one evening
and agreed they could produce a better one than those under consideration. A group, including Johnson, Kennedy,
McClellan, Cox, Freedman, and others from time to time,
continued to negotiate changes from these versions on the
Senate floor. In addition, several liberal Republican senators were reconsidering the bill of rights in light of its more
undesirable features. Senator Thomas Kuchel of California,
the minority whip, joined the group of Democrats huddled
on the Senate floor to draft revisions and left with a copy of
their work. That afternoon a bipartisan group including
Kuchel, George Aiken, Javits, Church, Clark, and Clifford
Case, Republican from New Jersey, met in Dirksen's office.
Out of this meeting came the so-called Kuchel Compromise.

When Kuchel presented his bipartisan compromise, the
reaction was so intense that one senator booed him and
later in the cloakroom took a swing at him. The bill of
rights had wounded Kennedy's presidential candidacy and
now the wound was being treated by the minority whip!
But it was obvious to everyone that a revision was necessary or the labor spokesmen would do everything possible
to prevent passage of a labor bill in the Senate. Senator
Styles Bridges, chairman of the Republican Policy Committee, raised a point of order that the matter had already
been voted on, but Vice-President Nixon ruled that the revisions were in order because they included contiguous
material and the changes were substantially different from
McClellan's original version. Kuchel defended his compromise by admitting he had voted for the bill of rights but
without reading it. The next day he and other senators read
what they had approved and decided "there were provisions which were imperfectly drawn, which should be improved, and changed." Kuchel's compromise was supported
by the AFL-CIO, southern senators, the Democratic lead-

ership, and McClellan himself, and it passed by a vote of seventy-seven to fourteen. The qualifying language made a union member's participation in union nominating, elections, and referenda meetings "subject to reasonable rules and regulations," and all rights were subject to the union's right to "adopt and enforce reasonable rules as to the responsibility of every member toward the organization as an institution and to his refraining from conduct that would interfere with its performance of its legal or its contractual obligations."[24] After settling this controversy, the Senate approved the Kennedy bill on 25 April by a vote of ninety to one, with Goldwater remaining steadfast against it.[25]

Passage of this bill by the Senate is a good example of how legislation ought not to be written. Laws should be drafted in committee and not "under the white hot glare of scores and scores of frenzied lawyers" on the floor of the Senate, where emotions were intense. Senators quickly realized their mistake in voting for a proposal they had never seen, let alone read and studied. Liberal Democrats, if they moved to strike the bill of rights, found themselves in the position of urging segregated unions; southern Democrats had to reverse themselves or risk being labeled integrationists at home. And none of them wanted to help communists join unions. Senator McClellan, a southern segregationist, had put his party in a deep dilemma. Oddly enough, the Democrats were saved from their embarrassment by a Republican, and a Republican leader at that.[26]

Edward McCabe, the White House liaison, who was directing the Republican efforts to enact labor reform legislation, was not amused by Kuchel's actions. He believed it was unnecessary for Kuchel to relieve the Democrats of their dilemma. Several Democrats were ready to take the lead in revising the bill of rights, and Kuchel's volunteering to do so took them off the hook. The Republican argument that if Kuchel did not take action the Senate would not approve any labor bill was nonsense, according to McCabe.

Without Kuchel's compromise, the Senate might have re-committed the bill with instructions. In that case, McCabe said, "we would have had the prize political picture of a Democratic Senate afraid to offend unions by adopting even part of McClellan's program." But, unfortunately, "Kuchel volunteered to break a solid Republican front, and then 'skillfully' mounted both horns of the Democrats' historic dilemma—the race issue, and their subservience to union bosses."[27] Attention to labor reform legislation now shifted to the House of Representatives.

6. The Two Sides Gird for Battle

More labor reform bills were introduced in Congress in 1959 than in any year since 1947. Almost fifty measures were presented, most of them in the House of Representatives. Early in the year both labor and management and Democrats and Republicans began developing strategies for pressing the particular proposal they desired through the House to strengthen or weaken the Senate-passed Kennedy bill.

President Eisenhower was determined to get a labor reform bill from Congress that contained the points he had asked for in 1958 and again in 1959. By 1959 his White House staff was functioning efficiently under its new chief, Wilton "Jerry" Persons. The administration strategists decided to portray the Senate bill as too weak and to substitute a tough bill in the House that would draw bipartisan support from the conservative coalition.

As usual, labor leaders were divided, with John L. Lewis demanding no labor reform legislation and repeal of the Wagner and Taft-Hartley acts and Walter Reuther supporting any and all efforts to rid the labor movement of corruption. One morning in June Reuther and George M. Harrison of the railway clerks union paid a call on Sam Rayburn to get his assessment of what action the House would take that session. They asked the Speaker to produce a bill that was "softer" than the Kennedy measure. Rayburn thought their suggestions were "too theoretical" and later said he could recognize at least ten factions in labor organizations and each one wanted different legislation.[1]

Within the AFL-CIO there was disagreement and dissension. The machinists, the steelworkers, and the communications workers wanted no bill at all and were supported by the independent United Mine Workers and teamsters. The building trades, as usual, were insisting on Taft-Hartley sweeteners. The auto workers wanted a labor reform bill on the order of the Kennedy proposal, although not quite so tough, and thought it should be enacted soon before public opinion was aroused sufficiently to demand a stronger measure.

In May the executive council of the AFL-CIO met again to determine strategy. Even though the council had supported the Kennedy bill and had helped draft parts of it, it now announced that it opposed the bill and preferred one that was "anticorruption but not antiunion." It was opposed to the amendments the Senate had added to the Kennedy bill, especially the bill of rights. The council declared that the Kennedy measure invited litigation, would be a source of conflict between federal and state laws, constituted an improper interference with legitimate union activities, and contained criminal sanctions that probably were unconstitutional. As the *New York Times* reported, even that "strong champion of clean unions" David Dubinsky opposed McClellan's bill of rights.[2]

Undoubtedly, the political activities of the teamsters at that time affected this decision. Soon after the Senate approved the Kennedy bill, the teamsters began actively to let congressmen know of their opposition to the proposal and launched a propaganda campaign within local unions. Vice-President Harold Gibbons of St. Louis and his legal adviser, Sidney Zagri, held a series of breakfasts at the Congressional Hotel in Washington to which they invited twenty-five to thirty congressmen at a time to hear their views. These meetings, which included some 250 representatives, were highly effective. Zagri, a graduate of UCLA and Harvard, was described as "a master of low pressure sweet reasonableness." At these meetings he called attention to weaknesses in the Kennedy bill from the teamsters' viewpoint and made suggestions for improving it. He also urged postponing action for a year to allow inflamed sentiment to cool off. One congressman described his presentation as "probably one of the best lobbying jobs ever done." Even Minority Leader Charles Halleck declared, "It looks like we won't have a labor bill this session."[3]

According to *Newsweek*, the teamster campaign scared the AFL-CIO into changing its position on labor reform. Jimmy Hoffa taunted George Meany that he should join the teamsters in their opposition to the Kennedy measure unless the AFL-CIO president was "stupid or else a strike-breaker." As one AFL-CIO labor leader noted, "Those Teamsters are all over the Hill fighting the bill. If it is killed they will take credit for it—unless we do something—and Jimmy Hoffa's prestige will go up with a lot of our own people." Yet the teamsters became too heavy-handed with the House Committee on Education and Labor, and their lobbying activities backfired.[4]

Management groups also were busy propagandizing and lobbying for their views on labor reform legislation. They were much more united than were labor leaders and thus more effective. They were more coordinated because Robert Gray, cabinet secretary, served as the clearing center for management activities. During the summer months, when labor legislation was developing in the House of Representatives, Edward McCabe was busy, often almost literally day and night, meeting with congressional leaders and promoting the administraion's program, so it was decided that Gray would serve as coordinator for management support to free McCabe for his work. McCabe thought Gray did an excellent job in this role.[5]

Management activities centered on taking advantage of the McClellan Committee revelations and arousing public opinion to demand that Congress control union corruption. Business groups made a list of congressmen who had won their seats in 1958 by a close margin and had never voted on an important labor bill. They refined the list to include about fifty who wanted a labor reform bill but were not committed to any particular measure. They then began a campaign in those congressmen's districts to arouse constituents to flood their congressmen with mail demanding that they vote for tough labor reform legislation. They also effectively used the television drama, "Sound of Violence," an hour-long show about union hoodlums in jukebox racketeering that had appeared on the Armstrong Circle Theatre in April 1959. The president of the Small Business Men's Association noted that "never before has the real meaning of both organizational picketing and secondary boycotts been so graphically and understandably depicted." Associates and employees of that organization were encouraged to watch the retelecast and then wire or write their congressman "of their feelings with regard to labor legislation." This campaign was part of Gray's job "to muster public support and channel it to a substitute bill when such a bill might emerge" and was highly effective.[6]

White House strategists, meanwhile, were preparing legislation that would encompass Eisenhower's labor philosophy. The cabinet was sharply divided on this issue. Postmaster General Arthur Summerfield supported tough labor legislation, as did interim Secretary of Commerce Lewis Strauss. When the Democratic-controlled Senate refused to confirm the appointment of Strauss, Frederick Mueller took his place, and he too pressed for a strong labor law. Secretary of Labor James Mitchell was a good spokesman for labor in the administration and also a very capable voice for the administration to labor leaders, and he was generally sympathetic to the plight of labor leaders in regard to reform legislation. He was thus in the uncomfortable position of having to help develop labor legislation his boss wanted, knowing that his constituency would find it unacceptable. As Edward McCabe put it, Mitchell was the official spokesman for the Eisenhower administration on labor matters, yet the labor bill was not under his management but was being developed and directed by McCabe.

Newsweek reported, in exaggerated terms, that only the possibility of getting the Republican vice-presidential nomination kept Mitchell in the cabinet. "Mitchell has recently lost several other Cabinet fights over more liberal labor policies he favors," the magazine declared. He would have "resigned last week" if his choice, Stuart Rothman, had not been named general counsel for the NLRB. But Mitchell was being touted in many quarters as a possible vice-presidential candidate, and he would certainly not be on the ticket with Richard Nixon in 1960 if he resigned from Eisenhower's cabinet. Developments in the House Committee on Education and Labor as it was writing a labor bill convinced McCabe and the White House staff that the best way to promote Eisenhower's program was to write a new bill incorporating the president's ideas and have it introduced as a substitute measure. To be successful, it would need bipartisan support from the conservative coalition.[7]

There were several congressmen who would play key roles in the passage of the new labor law. Sam Rayburn, Speaker of the House, was foremost on this list. "Mr. Sam," as he was affectionately called, was an institution unto himself. The eighth of eleven children of a cotton-farming family in northeast Texas, Rayburn served in the state legislature for six years before being elected to Congress in 1912. He became a liberal Democrat, supporting the programs of Woodrow Wilson, Franklin Roosevelt, Harry Truman, and, later, John Kennedy. He was elected Speaker of the House in 1940 and by 1959 had occupied that position longer than any man in history. Short, heavyset, and bald, Mr. Sam ran the House of Representatives with a friendly irascibility and had the respect of everyone. He was a bachelor who had been married very briefly as a young man; the House of Representatives was his family, and he devoted his life to it. As he once said, "I love this House. It is my life." Rayburn was convinced that it was vital for the Democrats to enact a labor reform law if they were to do well in the elections of 1960, and they should pass it in 1959 and not wait until the election year. He assigned his strategists, Lee Metcalf, and especially Richard Bolling, the task of shepherding a labor bill through the Committee on Education and Labor and the House of Representatives.

Charles Halleck, Phi Beta Kappa graduate of Indiana University, came to the House in 1935 as the representative of Jasper County, Indiana. He had the reputation of being one of the "roughest, most highly skilled infighters in U.S. politics." As he put it, "I am a gut fighter." This seamy-faced, stumpy, blue-eyed man often swallowed his conservative instincts to serve the interests of his party. With him leading the House Republicans and Dirksen leading in the Senate, Eisenhower soon reported that his weekly legislative meetings were "getting to be so much fun, they are running overtime." He once called Halleck "a political genius," and the two worked well together on a legislative program during Eisenhower's last two years in office.[8]

"Judge" Howard W. Smith was known as the leader of the conservative southern Democrats. A member of the Byrd machine of Virginia, Smith was elected to Congress in 1930 and was appointed to the powerful Rules Committee. When he became committee chairman he quietly and effectively used parliamentary tactics to throttle liberal legislation in the House and to promote bills desired by the conservative coalition. Under his guidance, the Rules Committee, in effect, became the third house of Congress and was a critical factor in getting any legislation through the House of Representatives.

Graham Barden, a southern gentleman from the old school, was chairman of the Committee on Education and

Labor. A lawyer from North Carolina, Barden was elected
to Congress in 1934 and during the New Deal became part
of the conservative coalition that Judge Smith and the Republican leadership could assemble on labor legislation,
economic issues, social policies, and civil rights. Many of
his committee members considered him dictatorial, but he
was also a master of delay, using the colorful local story to
give members time to rethink their positions and to compromise their differences.

Clare Hoffman was the senior Republican member of
the Committee on Education and Labor and had wanted for
years to get his name on a major labor law. But he was considered much too antiunion, and to have his support often
hurt one's cause more than it helped. Carroll Kearns,
elected to Congress from Pennsylvania in 1954, introduced
the administration's labor bill in January 1959. The law
that finally passed in 1959 would have borne his name except that he had a drinking problem and the administration
was afraid to trust him to shepherd the bill through
Congress.[9]

Instead, Robert P. Griffin, a junior Republican from
Michigan, was chosen by the administration to be its
spokesman for a bipartisan bill. After military service
in World War II, Griffin graduated from the University
of Michigan School of Law and set up practice in Traverse
City. At that time the congressional district that included
Traverse City encompassed the industrialized area from
that city along the shore of Lake Michigan to Muskegon, a
region that both the teamsters and the UAW were actively
organizing. As a result, many companies were looking for
legal counsel. The young lawyer was the only one available in the vicinity who had had a course in labor law, and
he soon made himself "an overnight expert" on labor-
management relations by representing these companies in
writing contracts, holding elections, and other labor-management affairs. By the time he was elected to Congress in
1956, he had acquired considerable expertise in labor law

for a small-town lawyer, and he won a seat on the Committee on Education and Labor. During House debate on the labor bill, John Kennedy asked Charlie Halleck, "Where did you dig up that Bobby Griffin? He's a smart young man."[10]

Phil Landrum, Democrat from Georgia, was Griffin's cosponsor of this bipartisan legislation. Following military service in World War II, Landrum practiced law and was elected to Congress in 1952. He preferred either the Judiciary or Banking committees, but Georgia was already represented on both of them so he accepted nomination to the Education and Labor Committee. By 1959 he was chairman of the Subcommittee on Labor Standards. He insisted on having Robert Griffin as his cosponsor because, although he was a junior Republican, Griffin "knew the subject well, was a good lawyer, and a first-rate technician." In addition, the two agreed in philosophy on what a labor reform bill should contain. As the Committee on Education and Labor began its work, Landrum and Griffin "were more or less drawn together from the beginning." Both representatives were considered neither particularly pro- nor antilabor.[11]

The AFL-CIO's COPE rated the members of the House Labor Committee on voting on labor legislation as follows (Fr. denotes a freshman representative):

Democrats		*Republicans*	
Graham Barden	4-9	Carroll Kearns	6-6
Adam Clayton Powell	12-0	Clare Hoffman	0-13
Cleveland Bailey	7-4	Joe Holt	4-9
Carl Perkins	9-3	Stuyvesant Wainwright	7-6
Roy Wier	11-2	Peter Freylinghuysen	8-5
Carl Elliott	11-2	William Ayres	7-6
Phil Landrum	4-9	Robert P. Griffin	5-7
Edith Green	12-1	John Lafore, Jr.	1-3
James Roosevelt	13-0	Edgar Heistand	0-13
Herbert Zelenko	12-0	Albert H. Quie	0-2

Democrats

Frank Thompson	13-0
Stewart Udall	13-0
Elmer Holland	13-0
Ludwig Teller	11-0
John H. Dent	3-0
Roman C. Pucinski	Fr.
Dominick Daniels	Fr.
John Brademas	Fr.
Robert Giaimo	Fr.
James O'Hara	Fr.

In addition, Charles Halleck was ranked 2-7 and Howard Smith 2-11.[12]

In May, after it had denounced the Kennedy bill, the AFL-CIO held another strategy meeting. Several AFL-CIO vice-presidents and George Meany were present, as well as Andrew Biemiller, former congressman and currently chief AFL-CIO legislative representative, and James McDevitt, director of COPE. They invited Bolling and Metcalf, representing Rayburn, and Stewart Udall and Frank Thompson, Democrat from New Jersey, all of whom were ranked pro-labor by COPE, to the meeting. The congressmen warned them repeatedly during this strategy session that to defeat a strong labor law, efforts must be made to enact a reform bill that would satisfy public demand to control union corruption even if it contained some objectionable features. This advice was met with hostility and rejection. Bolling stated that he was uncertain that the Democrats could maintain "even that position in committee or on the floor," to which Meany responded that labor would prefer defeat to compromise. Bolling replied "with a smile that such an attitude would make it easier on all of us." Meany then visited Rayburn but received the same message from the Speaker.[13]

House hearings were held on labor legislation from 4 March to 10 June. Carl Perkins was chairman of the Subcommittee on Labor-Management Relations. The conservative coalition considered him too prolabor, so Graham Barden, chairman of the parent Committee on Education and Labor, ordered hearings to be held by a joint subcommittee composed of members of the Subcommittee on Labor-Management Relations and the Subcommittee on Labor Standards. Because Perkins outranked Landrum, Barden decided they would be cochairmen of the joint committee, thus "ensuring there would be strong conservative representation at the hearings." The joint committee permitted the various interest groups to state their opinions at the hearings. Secretary Mitchell endorsed the administration or Kearns bill. A number of witnesses were produced by local chambers of commerce who told "stories of abuse through denial of internal democracy" and other tales of racketeering. Meany presented the position of the AFL-CIO, John L. Lewis spoke for the UMW, and Sidney Zagri represented the teamsters.[14]

The full thirty-member Committee on Education and Labor then began meeting to develop a bill to take to the floor of the House. Barden called nineteen executive sessions to consider a labor bill. There were twenty Democrats on the committee and ten Republicans. Barden and Landrum supported the Republican position. Ten of the remaining Democrats endorsed the AFL-CIO stance. The remaining eight were prounion but believed a labor reform bill must be reported. Five of these, known as the "fearless five," played a crucial role in what followed in the committee and on the floor of the House.

Democrats Stewart Udall, Frank Thompson, Carl Elliott, James O'Hara of Michigan, and Edith Green of Oregon represented districts where organized labor was powerful. All except the freshman O'Hara had prolabor voting records. Bolling and Metcalf decided there would be endless wrangling if the joint subcommittee tried to write a bill, so they worked with these "fearless five," or "faithless five" as union leaders would soon call them, because they agreed with the Democratic leadership that the House should vote out a good labor reform bill or they might end up with a strong labor law. Sometimes these five supported the pro-AFL-CIO Democrats on the committee against the antilabor movement and at other times voted with the conservative twelve "to keep the bill's teeth from being entirely pulled." Congressman Roy Wier moved to give the joint subcommittee responsibility for writing a bill, which lost twenty to ten. Barden and Landrum joined the Republicans as expected, but so had eight other Democrats, including the fearless five, whom labor leaders had expected to be supportive. This meant that labor had failed to bottle up the bill in subcommittee and the full Committee on Education and Labor would draft a proposal. The committee, after some rather violent debate, decided to use the Kennedy bill as a basis for discussions.[15]

Teamsters representative Sidney Zagri began to put pressure on the fearless five. He called Arizona Democrats to tell them Udall was voting wrong. When Udall complained, he replied, "I'm going to get you in line." Frank Thompson began receiving anonymous telephone calls warning him, "You're antilabor and we're going to fix you." The teamster lawyer pressured the "ladylike" Edith Green to the point that she "went way out of character and told Zagri to go to hell." Even Sam Rayburn became testy. When he heard that Zagri and Jimmy Hoffa were claiming that he supported their bill, Rayburn exploded, "It's a damn lie." *Time* magazine thought this teamster effort would redound against them. "By sending in his persuader," *Time* noted, "Jimmy Hoffa gave congressmen a personal taste of his tactics, apparently firmed up their resolve to do something about them." Rayburn called in the representatives who were being pressured and promised them, especially the freshmen, that he would campaign for any of them who were "put in serious trouble by Zagri's efforts."[16]

The committee worked on the Kennedy bill for several weeks and made more than a hundred changes in it. The solicitor general for the Department of Labor thought the committee improved the bill by rewriting some of the badly drafted language. Despite pressure from unions, the committee decided by a seventeen to thirteen vote to retain the provision that tightened up the Taft-Hartley loopholes on secondary boycotts and picketing. But the committee also decided to reverse the Denver building trades doctrine and legitimize common situs picketing. This was done primarily to split the building trades unions from the teamsters. Building trades workers would never consider a law to be antiunion if it solved their greatest problem. At this point Halleck expressed his concern at a legislative meeting at the White House that if the House bill were to get bogged down in committee, or if the Rules Committee delayed it, the Speaker would repeat his performance of 1958 and "throw the Senate bill at them under suspension of the rules, so it was essential to get *a* bill out." He also expressed the belief that "the chances of substituting a strong bill are better if the bill on the floor is weak." At this meeting the president was asked if he would make a speech on television supporting a labor reform bill. Eisenhower, who preferred to keep a low political profile, responded that he would "if he could keep it nonpartisan."[17]

As a result of this strategy meeting, Halleck persuaded Rayburn to join forces with him to get a bill reported to the House. Halleck thought he could deliver all ten Republican votes if necessary. When the final vote was taken in committee, ten Democrats supported the committee bill, and it passed sixteen to fourteen, with six Republicans voting yea, primarily to get a bill on the floor for debate. In supporting the committee bill, the faithful five, acording to *Time*, "had marched uphill into the muzzle of Big Labor's biggest guns in one of the 86th Congress' bloodiest unsung battles." The Speaker asked Graham Barden to sponsor the "battle-scarred" bill. This is the usual procedure for a bill that has been changed substantially in committee, and it would also remove a very influential congressman from the conservative coalition. Barden refused, saying he intended to support a substitute measure. The *New York Times* took his refusal to sponsor the bill to mean that the conservative coalition "would make a strong fight to amend it."[18] As it turned out, the newspaper was wrong; the coalition instead would support a tougher substitute proposal. One of the faithful five, Carl Elliott of Alabama, agreed to sponsor the committee bill.

The House report that accompanied the Elliott bill was an unusual one. Only the faithful five had kind words for it, calling it "a fair and effective instrument of labor-management reform." The committee chairman noted that he had voted for it so the House could debate it, but "it fails in so many respects to provide the remedies which are so urgently needed to correct major abuses" revealed by the McClellan Committee over the last three years. Liberal Democrats on the committee labeled it "punitive." Landrum and Griffin called it "woefully inadequate" and promised that their substitute bill would restore the "teeth" in the Senate-passed measure that had been extracted in the House committee. Clare Hoffman included "additional views" in the report. He pointed out that there had been no hearings or discussions on the substitute bill and it seemed to be made up of parts of the McClellan bill, the administration proposal, the Kearns measure, and several others. "Notwithstanding its illegitimacy," he would support the Elliott bill if the House did not amend it substantially.[19]

Sam Rayburn took, for him, the unusual step of issuing a public statement in support of the Elliott bill. The committee proposal "does a splendid job," he said. "It controls racketeering, hot cargo, and extortion or shakedown picketing." Rayburn stated that he was "as much against racketeering as anybody could be" and the committee bill covered this problem "in a fine fashion." Everyone, of course, had to be against racketeering.[20]

When asked his opinion of the Elliott bill, Everett Dirksen gave the administration response that the Senate bill

was "weak" and "inadequate." It failed to meet the need
for labor reform "and so in proportion as the House waters
down the Senate version, we get even further from the goal
we hope to realize."[21] Edward McCabe and the White
House staff decided that, rather than try to amend the bill
on the House floor to strengthen it, a substitute measure
should be introduced that embodied the administration's
ideas.

Political considerations dominated the thinking of the
administration's strategists. The Democrats controlled
Congress by huge majorities. If the administration bill
were to pass Congress, it would require a large number of
southern Democratic votes, along with solid Republican
support. Therefore, it would have to be promoted as a bipartisan measure, not an administration proposal. Widespread public support would also be necessary. The
sponsors, then, should be congressmen not known to be
antilabor and with personalities that could rally support,
both in the House and among the general public. McCabe
discussed this problem with Judge Smith of the Rules
Committee, Graham Barden, and House Minority Leader
Halleck. At Smith's insistence, they went down the se-
niority list to Phil Landrum of Georgia, and Halleck went
way down the Republican list and picked Robert Griffin of
Michigan to cosponsor the "nonpartisan" measure. Subsequently, it was always referred to as the Landrum-Griffin
bill and never the reverse to emphasize that it was
bipartisan.[22]

On 27 July, four days after the committee reported the
Elliott bill, the Landrum-Griffin proposal was introduced
in the House of Representatives. Three days later, John
Shelley, Democrat from California, introduced the measure supported by the AFL-CIO. When asked about the
Landrum-Griffin bill at a news conference, President Eisenhower called it "a tremendous improvement" over the
Kennedy and Elliott proposals. He commended the "nonpartisan" sponsors, saying that their measure "comes a

long way closer to meeting" his January requests than did the other labor reform bills in Congress.[23]

On 2 August George Meany sent a letter to all congressmen asking them to "soften" the Elliott bill or to abandon all attempts at passing labor reform legislation that session. That same day the ten Republican members of the House Committee on Education and Labor wrote the president, asking for his public support of the Landrum-Griffin bill. Meanwhile, Robert Gray set in motion "an all out campaign to support the substitute bill by name." This campaign included newspaper advertisements, television shows featuring labor violence, and favorable statements by McClellan (who supported the Landrum-Griffin measure), and Landrum and Griffin in spot advertisements for key areas of the country. In addition, it was arranged for Landrum and Griffin to appear on the "Today" show, a very popular morning television program.[24]

A comparison of the principal labor bills before the House in August 1959 demonstrates that the major difference lay in the last title of each proposal. Title I in all the bills contained the bill of rights. The Kennedy bill would punish violations with fines of $10,000 and/or two years in prison, whereas the Elliott bill limited fines to $1,000 and/or one year in prison. The Shelley measure merely specified the responsibility of union members not to abuse their rights. Title II required unions to file copies of their constitutions, by-laws, and financial operations with the secretary of labor. The Elliott bill exempted unions from this requirement if they had fewer than two hundred members or gross annual receipts of less than $20,000. The Landrum-Griffin bill did not exempt small unions from reporting. Title III limited trusteeships to legitimate union purposes and in both the Landrum-Griffin and Elliott proposals the trusteeship would be valid for eighteen months, whereas the Kennedy bill limited them to twelve months. Title IV required secret elections for union officers and established maximum terms for them. Removal procedures were to be provided for local officials in all four bills. Title V in the Elliott bill specified fiduciary responsibilities of union officials, required their bonding, prohibited loans of more than $2,500 to officers or union employees, forbade union payments of fines of employees who violated the law, and prohibited communists and convicts from holding union office or being employed by a union. In Title VI the Elliott bill made it a criminal offense to picket for "extortionate" purposes, as did the Landrum-Griffin and Kennedy measures. The primary difference was that the Kennedy bill would penalize offenses up to a $10,000 fine and/or two years in prison while Landrum-Griffin limited penalties to $1,000 and/or one year in prison. As George Reedy noted in a memorandum to Senate Majority Leader Lyndon Johnson comparing the various bills, the first six titles of each were substantially the same; "the differences . . . could be adjusted by reasonable men in the course of a leisurely afternoon."[25]

The principal differences in the measures came in Title VII, the Taft-Hartley amendments. Among the subjects covered here were no-man's land on which the Elliott and Shelley bills would require the NLRB to assert jurisdiction, Landrum-Griffin would give jurisdiction to the states, and the Kennedy bill would give jurisdiction to the states but they must apply federal law. The Elliott, Shelley, and Kennedy proposals would permit prehire contracts and require union membership after seven rather than thirty days. The Elliott bill would permit common situs picketing. Landrum-Griffin would permit prehire contracts only where there was a prior history of collective bargaining and no provision was made for common situs picketing. Elliott, Shelley, and Kennedy would permit economic strikers to vote while Landrum-Griffin would prohibit elections during a strike for six months after a petition was filed by someone other than the bargaining representatives or for twelve months after a petition was filed by the employer. The Kennedy bill would exclude service assistants as "supervisors" while the other three bills had no provision on this matter. The Shelley bill had no provision for hot cargo contracts while the other three proposals made them an unfair labor practice. Landrum-Griffin would also make it an unfair practice to threaten to strike any company to force it to cease doing business with another person. Finally, the Elliott and Kennedy bills would make organizational picketing an unfair practice if another union had been recognized by the employer, or a valid election had been held in the previous twelve months, or the union was able to demonstrate "sufficient showing of interest" by the employees, or picketing continued for up to thirty days and no election petition was filed. The Shelley bill had no provision for organizational picketing. Obviously, in terms of union objections, according to George Reedy, "the real sticklers are the secondary boycott and organizational picketing provisions." The Landrum-Griffin bill did not contain any Taft-Hartley sweeteners. According to Edward McCabe, the administration planners followed the same strategy that Congressman Hartley had followed twelve years previously: they had inserted tough provisions in the House bill, knowing the Senate bill would be softer, and they would have something to compromise away in conference. So the Landrum-Griffin proposal contained "a heavy bit of medicine in the House knowing that we could water it down with the Senate formula and we would come out with what we wanted," McCabe stated.[26]

As the House prepared to debate the bills, Bolling met with Andrew Biemiller and pointed out that there was no way to block both the Elliott and Landrum-Griffin measures. One or the other would get through the House. The AFL-CIO must begin to work for support for the Elliott proposal. The Democratic leadership and the union representatives then worked together to count their support in the House. In Bolling's words, "the result of the first count sobered everyone." Support for the Landrum-Griffin bill ran ahead of the Elliott measure, although a large number of congressmen had not yet made their decisions. Robert Gray and his minions in the U.S. Chamber of Commerce and the National Association of Manufacturers began stepping up their pressure on the fifty or more waverers. Again in Bolling's words, "strong members blanched under their pressure." He told of Erwin Mitchell, Democrat from Georgia, who was subjected to "round the clock harassment" but remained loyal to the Democratic leadership. His first term was his last one, and he left Congress in ill health as a result of this unhappy episode in his life.[27]

Edward McCabe met at a luncheon session with a number of management representatives to discuss the general content of the Landrum-Griffin bill and the administration's strategy. When some of them began specifying changes they wanted made, he countered that the administration was going to press for the possible, not the ideal law, and they should leave this up to the professionals on Capitol Hill. They could best assist by quietly working with Robert Gray's people in putting pressure on congressmen from their districts. Above all, they should not become conspicuous like the union representatives but use their influence as subtly as possible. Finally, they should continually reiterate that "the people" were demanding a strong law, Landrum-Griffin was a strong bill, and it was bipartisan.[28]

For the previous two months in legislative and staff meetings it had been emphasized that the president should make a special plea for a strong labor reform law. Eisenhower repeatedly agreed but told his staff that timing would be crucial. They were to gauge how the legislation was progressing on Capitol Hill to determine when his speech would be most effective. They told him that a week to ten days before the House vote would be best because the people would then have time to write or call their congressmen and express their opinions.

Legislative strategists grew even more convinced that the president should speak out on the subject when they saw the public reaction to Robert Kennedy's appearances on television. In late July Kennedy was a guest on the "To-night" show hosted by Jack Parr. Following his introduc-tion, Kennedy spoke informally and movingly about corruption in the labor movement and the need for reform legislation, although he did not specifically endorse any bill pending before the House. His obvious sincerity in ap-pealing to the viewers to write their congressmen and ex-press their views resulted in a flood of mail to senators and representatives. Everett Dirksen reported receiving as many as two thousand letters in one day, all of them prompted by Kennedy's appeal. Four days after his first ap-pearance, young Kennedy appeared on "Meet the Press" and made another emotional plea for a labor reform law.[29]

Congressmen noted a significant difference in this mail. Previously they had received messages that were obviously "inspired" or form letters produced by unions. Now they were receiving mail written "in pencil on dime-store pa-per" with faulty syntax and misspellings. *Newsweek*, in describing this deluge, observed that Robert Kennedy, "like a dentist probing with a drill, really touched the raw nerve ends of the people." At the next legislative meeting following Kennedy's TV appearances, Eisenhower an-nounced that he would make a radio and television pre-sentation on labor legislation, a most unusual step for him to take because his presidential style was to maintain a low profile and give the impression he was "above poli-tics." As *Time* magazine put it, never before in his presi-dency had he thrown "his great public prestige into a raging congressional fight" as he now planned to do.[30]

Edward McCabe spent two days writing a speech draft. During that time he received two telephone calls. The postmaster general and the secretary of commerce asked if he was getting any "static" from the Department of Labor. If so, they said, "let us know and we will weigh in with the President so this thing can be done the way it's set up and the way you are doing." McCabe assured them he had re-ceived no pressure from James Mitchell.[31]

On 6 August President Eisenhower addressed the nation

on all the major radio and television networks. He presented himself as being above politics, saying that the need for labor reform was an issue "above any partisan political consideration." He defined racketeering and corruption in labor-management affairs as "a national disgrace." Most union officials were honest and the corruption was limited to a minority, he noted, but this damage "to the American public cannot be tolerated." The president particularly denounced blackmail picketing, secondary boycotts, and the current legal status of the no-man's-land issue. He labeled the Kennedy bill "ineffective" and the Elliott proposal "even less effective." Then he went one step beyond Robert Kennedy's appeal by specifically endorsing the Landrum-Griffin bill as "bipartisan." "I am not a candidate for office," he reminded his listeners, and "I do not seek the support of any special interests." He concluded by expressing the hope that Congress would "be fully responsive to an overwhelming demand."[32]

This address stimulated an even greater flood of mail than Robert Kennedy's appearances. For the first time in his presidency, the most popular incumbent president in history made a public appeal for legislation he wanted and specified the bill by name. "Not since Harry Truman fired Gen. Douglas MacArthur," Newsweek announced, "had Congress seen such a deluge of mail." Americans had been asked by their beloved president to lend their support to labor reform and they responded. Both Phil Landrum and Robert Griffin were convinced that this address turned the tide for their bill. The overwhelming response and pressure on wavering congressmen brought their legislation through Congress.[33]

Democrats, of course, immediately labeled the address as partisan. Erwin Mitchell called the Landrum-Griffin bill "the greatest political hoax in many years." The Republicans knew that if the House passed it, the Senate would not, he asserted, and thus they would have a hot political issue in 1960. The Republicans would blame the Democratic-controlled Senate for not controlling Jimmy Hoffa. Mike Mansfield, the Democratic whip from Montana, demanded equal time to respond to Eisenhower. All of the networks refused, however, except the Mutual radio network, which allowed Sam Rayburn air time. Rayburn stated that Congress needed to pass "a strong effective bill to put an end to these criminal activities" in labor-management relations. But "powerful interests" were afield, and they were "using the public demand for a cleanup of racketeering as a smoke screen behind which they can impose crippling restraints on the honest, legitimate interests of the working man." Congress had a choice "between the Republican-backed bill" and the Elliott proposal. The Republican measure would put the government "so heavily on the side of management that . . . it would constitute a genuine injustice," he asserted, and he called for support for the Elliott bill "as the road of reason and fair play." But few Americans heard Rayburn's appeal and it generated little public response. As Richard Bolling noted, no Speaker has the impact of the president, especially a very popular one.[34]

A few days after Eisenhower's address, Joseph Loftus, writing for the *New York Times*, analyzed the president's speech. The three areas in which the president said action was needed, he pointed out, "figured in the McClellan Committee disclosures of power abuses in a secondary way," and the committee's indictment of Hoffa contained no mention of the three points. "All three issues . . . figure in the labor-management power struggle," he observed, and "are travelling as reform measures." He declared that the president had misinformed the public by using an example of a secondary boycott that was "already outlawed by the Taft-Hartley Act."[35] But the president's speech was the deciding factor for several wavering congressmen who would ultimately make the difference in the voting in the House of Representatives.

7. The Forces Engage

Labor reform legislation was the hottest topic debated in the first session of the Eighty-sixth Congress, but a related issue, civil rights, was also a major problem at that time. The next year, in the second session, it would be the principal subject of discussion and would culminate in the Civil Rights Act of 1960. The two issues often were closely intertwined because the conservative coalition found common agreement on them and votes on the two were used as trade-offs. Southern Democrats would support northern Republicans with labor reform legislation if the Republicans would help ward off civil rights laws. These were also opposites, of course, representing law versus no law.

In the first session of the Eighty-sixth Congress Emanuel Celler, chairman of the House Committee on the Judiciary, announced that he was certain his committee could report a civil rights bill that year. By the time his committee reported to the House in early August, though, he had lost significant Republican support, and he denounced the "unholy alliance" of Republicans and southern Democrats who had emasculated his civil rights bill in committee. Following passage of the labor reform bill, Celler lamented that apparently Judge Smith had civil rights legislation bottled up in the Rules Committee for the remainder of the session. He was convinced that a "deal" had been struck on civil rights and labor reform legislation, and there was much muttering and whispering in the Eighty-sixth Congress about this deal. Judge Smith also kept the labor reform bill in the Rules Committee long enough for Eisenhower to make his speech and the public response to arrive in Congress before debate on the Elliott bill began.[1]

The House had three labor reform bills to consider. The Elliott bill, produced by the committee from the Kennedy proposal, was supported by the Democratic leadership and opposed by the AFL-CIO. Sam Rayburn was supporting it as staunchly as any measure he had endorsed during the decade. Richard Bolling decided to try to keep the Elliott bill from being amended and to defeat the second proposal, the Landrum-Griffin bill supported by the administration, so the House would have no choice but to accept the Elliott bill. The third measure, sponsored by John Shelley, Democrat from California and a former member of the AFL-CIO, and James Roosevelt, also a Democrat from California, had the support of liberal Democrats and organized labor but had no chance of passage because it was considered too soft to curb Jimmy Hoffa.

The Democratic leadership encountered at least two problems during debate on labor reform legislation. Carl Elliott's health was one. The person whose name is on a bill "often assumes a decisive importance," Bolling noted, and having Elliott sponsor the committee bill was a definite asset. Elliott represented a rural district in Alabama and was a sincere man, respected by his colleagues and especially influential with his southern friends. The Democratic leadership counted on him to prevent the conservative coalition from coalescing completely. But just before the debate began, Elliott was hospitalized with a severe gall bladder attack that required surgery. Stewart Udall of Arizona, one of the faithful five, had to assume the task of managing the committee bill on the House floor.[2]

Second, the Democratic leadership went into the debate with a hole card that they thought, when produced at the proper time, would drive southern support away from the Landrum-Griffin bill. Archibald Cox gave the administration measure a thorough examination and discovered a potential "sleeper" in it. Language in Title I, if pursued through a series of references in the proposal, could be interpreted as a strong civil rights clause. One hundred copies of this analysis were prepared and kept in Bolling's office. Cox stated that the measure incorporated the civil rights section of the Fourteenth Amendment and would require integrated union locals with integrated social activities throughout the country. At the exact moment when the Elliott bill could no longer be amended, copies of this analysis would be presented to southern congressmen, who then would have no choice but to vote against Landrum-Griffin and support the Elliott bill.[3] This tactic backfired, however, because it was disclosed prematurely.

Debate on the labor reform proposals began on 11 August. Bills are debated on either a closed rule that prohibits amendments or an open rule permitting changes within the time limit set for debate. Judge Smith's Rules Committee reported the labor bill with an open rule. Smith then explained the parliamentary situation to his colleagues:

Mr. Speaker, we have a very remarkable situation here today. We have a rule for the consideration of a labor bill. We have two proposed substitutes to the labor bill. And to be as brief as I can about the rule, it is, I will say, a wide-open rule under the rules of the House. The so-called committee bill will first be considered. When it is read for amendment, at the conclusion of the first section, the gentleman from Georgia will offer the so-called Landrum-Griffin bill as an amendment. It will then be in order to offer the so-called Shelley-Roosevelt bill as a substitute for the Landrum-Griffin amendment. It will then be in order to have one amendment each to the Shelley-Roosevelt substitute and the Landrum-Griffin amendment pending at the same time. The Landrum-Griffin amendment will be perfected by whatever amendment will be offered before any vote is taken on any amendments to the Shelley-Roosevelt substitute. Then that amendment will be perfected. Then the Roosevelt substitute will be, I hope, voted down. Then the Landrum-Griffin bill will, I hope, be voted up. If that occurs we will then be at the end of the road. That would then be reported back to the House and the House would vote on the Landrum-Griffin amendment. If that is defeated, in the Committee of the Whole, of course, the committee bill will be open to the much-needed amendments to make it a good labor-management bill. When all that is done to get it to conference, it will be necessary to substitute the Senate bill. The provisions of the Senate bill will be stricken out and whatever the result of the House deliberations is will be inserted in Senate bill, S. 1555. Then the House will appoint conferees. So much for the rule.[4]

The Committee of the Whole is a parliamentary device whereby the House resolves itself into committee, debate time is limited, one hundred members constitute a quorum, and there are no recorded votes. Supporters of the administration bill hoped that during that time their proposal would be accepted as a substitute for the committee measure. The Committee of the Whole would then resolve itself as the House again, the Democratic leadership would demand a roll call of the amendments added by nonrecorded votes in the Committee of the Whole, and, at that point, they would give the southerners the "civil rights" analysis. They would then desert the Landrum-Griffin bill, which at that point, could not be amended.[5]

Debate time was controlled by the conservative coalition. Graham Barden divided his three hours equally among the Democrats with one each going to the Elliott, Landrum-Griffin, and Shelley supporters. Carroll Kearns allotted all the Republican time to Griffin's supporters. When the Republican leadership chose Robert Griffin to sponsor the administration bill, he was jumped over Kearns and Clare Hoffman, each of whom wanted very much to have his name on a labor reform bill. Kearns sadly accepted the decision that it would be Griffin, and he generously led the floor fight for the good of his party; rejection rankled Hoffman, and his outrage would emerge at the end of the debate.

When complex legislation is being considered, debate becomes very important. Congressman Ray Madden, Democrat from Indiana and member of the Rules Committee, lamented: "I venture to say that more than half the Members in this House have not read or mentally digested in toto any of the three long and complex bills now under consideration by this body."[6] In this situation the reputations of the leaders and debaters for veracity and for their knowledge of the subject matter are crucial in swaying opinions.

Even before debate began, congressional tempers were rising and the atmosphere in the House was tense. During discussions in the Rules Committee when decisions were being made on reporting the Elliott bill to the floor, Congressman Madden touched off sparks in Phil Landrum. Madden, who represented the highly industrialized area of Gary, Indiana, and was a staunch prounion man, bitingly denounced the Landrum-Griffin bill as having been written by the National Association of Manufacturers.

> "You son of a . . . "Mr. Landrum began hotly.
> "What did you say?" demanded Madden.

The chairman finally restored order, and Landrum apologized. As the *New York Times* described it, the Shelley bill was killed on the first day of debate "in an atmosphere of rising tempers." Two debaters got out of hand and had to be called to order by their colleagues. At another time one congressman had to be physically restrained from attacking a colleague. The situation was best summed up when one congressman observed that they were debating the Congressional Retirement Act of 1959.[7]

The tenseness in the House prompted a pessimism in the Republican leadership. At a legislative meeting in the White House on 28 July, Charles Halleck observed that "the Landrum-Griffin substitute is the closest thing to the Administration position anywhere around," and he optimistically predicted that "it might attract 220 votes." (As it turned out, he undercounted by nine votes, and Halleck was a good House counter.) But two weeks later the minority leader pessimistically reported to the White House that "he expected a very difficult time in getting it approved." Probably his optimism dwindled because by the time debate opened the House of Representatives was swarming with labor lobbyists.[8]

Reporters exaggerated their numbers, but unions brought a great number of people to Washington to try to sway congressmen. In addition to its usual thirty-five lobbyists, the AFL-CIO put another hundred men to work on congressmen (one journal reported as many as two hundred AFL-CIO lobbyists). The teamsters also increased their numbers and at one point had four hundred lobbyists roaming the halls of Congress, buttonholing congressmen anywhere they could find them. During the debates congressmen increasingly spent more time on the floor of the House as "the only refuge" from union lobbyists on one hand and telephone calls and telegrams from management lobbyists on the other. Graham Barden accused Andrew Biemiller of "sticking his fingers in one member's face and saying 'Listen you, this is it. You're going to do this or else.' " Often this pressure backfired. *Time* reported a lobbyist for the bakers union warning Republican John Lindsay of New York, "we're going to have to work you over in 1960," with the result that Lindsay subsequently changed his vote to support Landrum-Griffin.[9]

Management and administration lobbyists also were very active, only in a more subdued, effective way. Ads in newspapers, letters to congressmen, telephone calls to wavering representatives from influential industrialists back home, individual discussions by congressional leaders and administrative spokesmen with the questionable fifty freshmen, all converged in the three days of debate to convince congressmen they had to vote for a strong bill—the Landrum-Griffin measure. The *Congressional Record* listed visits by Postmaster General Arthur Summerfield and Attorney General William Rogers to congressional offices during debates. Edward McCabe reported that Robert

Gray "did terribly well" in convincing management lobbyists not to make the mistake of union people and become "too vocal." Smith, Barden, and Halleck were carefully counting votes. If any were found wavering, they could expect a call from a cabinet member or, occasionally, from their finance chairman in their home district, reminding them that President Eisenhower very much wanted the Landrum-Griffin bill enacted. Judge Smith "worked his magic" lining up southern votes in the cloakrooms and by telephone.[10]

The six hours of debate took place on 11 to 13 August. The Elliott and Landrum-Griffin bills were similar in their first six titles; the greatest differences came in Title VII, the Taft-Hartley amendments. Supporters of the Elliott proposal made much of the point that a good part of the administration substitute was drawn from their measure. Landrum-Griffin supporters emphasized that their substitute constituted the "minimum" necessary for a reasonable labor reform law. They continued to refer to their bill as "moderate." The Democratic leadership stressed that the Republicans were pushing Landrum-Griffin with the idea that they could get it through the House but then the more liberal Senate would reject it. Thus the Democratic-controlled Congress would kill labor reform legislation and the Republicans would have their issue in 1960.

Metcalf produced a letter from Robert Kennedy that said the Elliott bill was the best for controlling corruption and racketeering exposed by the McClellan Committee, and the conservative coalition submitted a letter from McClellan, who disagreed with what he called "Kennedy's personal opinion" and expressed approval of the Landrum-Griffin bill. At the end of debate on 12 August, the Landrum-Griffin proposal was formally presented as a substitute for the Elliott measure and the Shelley bill was offered as a substitute for the substitute. The two substitutes were then opened to perfecting amendments.[11]

Adam Clayton Powell, the flamboyant Democrat from

Harlem, introduced an amendment to include civil rights provisions in the Landrum-Griffin bill. At this point James Roosevelt could not contain himself and rose to support Powell. Roosevelt noted that he had searched the Landrum-Griffin measure to find something in it worthy of his support. As Bolling sat stunned and speechless, Roosevelt informed southern congressmen that he had found "a silver lining" in section 210 of Landrum-Griffin. This provision gave the secretary of labor injunctive powers to protect the civil rights of union members against their union's actions. He had sprung the Democratic leadership's booby trap twenty-four hours too soon. This gave the conservative coalition the opportunity to clarify the civil rights issue while the measure could still be amended. William Cramer, Democrat from Florida, rose to explain that this problem, like the Civil Rights Act of 1957, was taken care of in section 608 of the proposal that provided for trial by jury in any criminal contempt cases. Also an amendment was later added to correct a section number, and this change clarified any civil rights problems with the bill. Powell's amendment was then rejected 215 to 160 and the Shelley bill was defeated 245 to 132.[12] The Committee of the Whole then rose and resolved itself into the House of Representatives for the day.

As final discussion opened on 13 August, with the House again sitting as a Committee of the Whole, some congressmen had to have the parliamentary situation explained to them again. If they adopted the Landrum-Griffin substitute, they could not go through it section by section but had to accept it in toto. But if it was defeated, the House then could go through the Elliott bill and amend it section by section. Liberal Democrats began pleading with union leaders to allow them to make minor perfecting changes in the Elliott bill to gain the support of wavering congressmen and defeat Landrum-Griffin. But remembering the undesirable changes made in the Kennedy bill when it was debated in the Senate, the AFL-CIO remained adamant. Now that the choice was between the Elliott bill and Landrum-Griffin, they foolishly said the Elliott proposal must be passed unchanged.[13]

At this point House Majority Whip John McCormack of Massachusetts began baiting Halleck. Speaker Rayburn had made an agreement with Halleck that the two would not participate in the debates. This was good for Rayburn because Halleck was most adept at parliamentary debating, and the Speaker did not want to engage him in a duel. It was also of great benefit to Halleck because he could then insist that Landrum-Griffin was a nonpartisan bill and he would not inject politics into it by debating. But it was terribly difficult for Halleck, who loved the rough and tumble of House debate, to keep quiet. McCormack observed that though the National Association of Manufacturers supported Landrum-Griffin, the bill still was not strong enough for management. During his thirty-one years in Congress, the NAM and the Chamber of Commerce had "opposed every progressive piece of legislation" he had seen. He thought there were perhaps twenty-five or thirty congressmen "who still have their minds open," and "most of them are on the Republican side." He further noted that Postmaster General Summerfield and Attorney General Rogers were, that very day, putting pressure on these representatives. Halleck managed to restrain his instincts to debate and refused to politicize the administration's bill.[14]

The House considered a number of amendments to the Landrum-Griffin proposal. Oren Harris, Democrat from Arkansas, proposed to exempt railroad workers because they were exempt from the Wagner and Taft-Hartley laws. This would "win over six Republicans who were under great pressure from railway unionists in their districts." The proposal was narrowly defeated 183 to 179. Clare Hoffman's amendments to prohibit strikes in public utilities and to bring unions under the antitrust laws also went down to defeat. John Dowdy, Democrat from Texas, of-

fered to change section 210 to 102. This was an inter-
polation of numbers and was referred to earlier by Congressman Cramer. This change was agreed to and definitely
elminated any civil rights problem in the bill. J. Carleton
Loser, Democrat from Tennessee, moved to reduce the
penalty on union hall disorders from $10,000 and/or two
years in prison to $1,000 and/or one year, which carried.
Democrat Barratt O'Hara of Illinois observed, "Looking to
my left I see so many troubled [Republican] faces, and
glimpse such agonizing signs of troubled consciences, so I
give the remainder of my time to them for a period of si-
lent prayer."[15] Following prayer it was time to vote in the
Committee of the Whole.

It was a teller vote and many congressmen were hanging
back to see which way the tide was going before moving forward to vote. Charlie Halleck noticed that Edith
Nourse Rogers, Republican from Massachusetts, was leaving
the floor. Although she was afraid to vote no on Landrum-
Griffin, she knew a yea vote would be unpopular in her district, and she decided to adjourn to the ladies room. Halleck sent Silvio Conte, also a Massachusetts Republican,
running after her. She saw him coming and dashed into the
restroom. Conte pounded on the door, shouting, "Edith,
come out! I know you are in there—Charlie orders you to
come out and vote." Mrs. Rogers remained in her sanctu-
ary, however, until the votes were counted.[16]

At the last minute Rayburn asked the Texas delegation,
"If you can't vote with us, would you consider not going
through the tellers on either side?" But Homer Thorn-
berry, a Lyndon Johnson man, went through the yea side
and a number who were waiting and watching then followed him. The tellers announced 215 ayes, 200 nos. The
conservative coalition had won. Kenneth McGuiness,
counsel for Robert Griffin and former counsel for the
NLRB, was present. He looked at his boss, and at that moment they both knew the Landrum-Griffin bill would be
enacted.[17] The Committee of the Whole then rose and re-

ported the Landrum-Griffin measure to the House of Representatives for a recorded vote. The recorded vote came out 229 to 201. Of the 434 eligible congressmen, 430 cast their votes, with four abstaining. When the votes were tallied the Democratic leadership discovered that all those listed as "doubtful" in their support of the Elliott bill had voted for the Landrum-Griffin measure.[18]

The administration-industrialist lobbyists could be pleased with their efforts because, of the 54 congressmen they had targeted as leaning toward a "softer bill," 23, or more than the fourteen-vote margin on the final tally, voted their way. One hundred southerners joined 126 Republicans on this vote, along with 3 Democrats from Kansas, Nebraska, and New Mexico (Kansas and Nebraska were right-to-work states). A short time later Senator Karl Mundt wrote Graham Barden to congratulate him on getting the bill through the House. He noted that when southern Democrats and rural Republicans "get going on a joint effort, 'We can run the country! Perhaps we should do it oftener!'"[19]

Every Republican who voted against the Kennedy-Ives bill in 1958 voted for the Landrum-Griffin substitute. The same was true for southern Democrats with the exception of Erwin Mitchell of Georgia, who was not in Congress in 1958, and he voted against Landrum-Griffin. The next year the Georgia Democratic leadership denied Mitchell renomination to the Eighty-seventh Congress. A congressman from New York asked a number of his southern colleagues why they voted for Landrum-Griffin. Their response was that they wanted it to become law "to prevent union interference with the industrialization of the South." There was an interesting irony that northern Republicans joined forces with southern Democrats to encourage industry to move from the North to the South.[20]

On this vote Sam Rayburn lost sixteen of the twenty-two Texans to the conservative coalition. Many news reporters attributed this loss to Lyndon Johnson, who told the Texans to "vote your district." Johnson's chief rival in the Senate for the Democratic presidential nomination, John Kennedy, stood to lose the most if Landrum-Griffin were enacted. Richard Bolling, who claimed he knew Rayburn's thinking on labor legislation better than anyone except Rayburn, supports this "plot" thesis although he admitted Rayburn could not always control the Texas delegation. But in his book *House Out of Order,* Bolling tells a story that undercuts his suspicions of a Johnson plot. After the vote on Landrum-Griffin, Bolling asked Rayburn if he could bring Udall, Metcalf, and Thompson to his "board of education" meeting that afternoon. Rayburn met every afternoon in his office with some of his fellow Texans, and Democratic leaders sometimes dropped in for bourbon and talk of politics. This day Mr. Sam said, "I can't stand to be with those Texans tonight," and did not hold his usual meeting. But the next evening he did meet with Bolling and the others, and when John McCormack came in he looked surprised to see who was present. "John," said the Speaker, "this time I thought for a change I'd like to be with the boys that are with me." When asked about this alleged Johnson plot, Landrum responded that when he thanked a Texan for his vote he replied, "Hell, Phil, don't thank me, thank all those folks in my district."[21] A combination of Jimmy Hoffa's corruption, Carl Elliott's gall bladder, James Roosevelt's premature disclosure of the civil rights issue, and Dwight Eisenhower's address, not Lyndon Johnson, had defeated John Kennedy's labor bill.

Following this vote, Clare Hoffman requested an engrossed copy. This was a privileged motion and caused a one-day delay in the final vote. Charlie Halleck was "outraged." He had just had complete victory in his hand, and now Hoffman was putting it in jeopardy. Halleck marched up to Hoffman's desk to explode at him. Hoffman was still furious at being bypassed in sponsorship of the administration bill and being allowed only one minute each instead of five to discuss his amendments that day, and he "unleashed a colorful blast at the Minority Leader and walked out." This created a problem because a motion to recommit must be made by someone opposed to the bill. The chair would first recognize the senior man on the Committee on Education and Labor (Barden, who supported Landrum-Griffin) and then the senior minority member (Kearns). Halleck talked to Kearns, and he agreed to make the motion because he saw the possibility of introducing another Kearns bill if the motion to recommit carried. His motion to recommit the next day lost 280 to 148. The Landrum-Griffin bill then passed the House 303 to 175. Seventy-five more congressmen hopped "on the speeding bandwagon" after labor released them to "vote your district to get re-elected next year."[22]

Conservatives saw the large final vote as a reflection of the public desire to curb union corruption, and they became overoptimistic. Senator Karl Mundt took the lead in trying to bypass the conference committee procedure and bring the Landrum-Griffin bill directly to the Senate floor for a vote. By taking advantage of the momentum that had built up for a tough bill, Mundt thought it would be possible to get the measure through the Senate without change. But he was unable to persuade "many Southern Democrats" to adopt this unusual procedure, and his efforts came to nought. The Kennedy and Landrum-Griffin bills then went to conference.[23]

The Speaker appoints the House conferees, and he usually takes the recommendation of the chairman of the committee with jurisdiction. Sam Rayburn appointed four Democrats—Barden, Landrum, Perkins, and Thompson—and three Republicans—Kearns, William Ayres, and Griffin. The manager for the Republicans, Griffin, made certain he always had Kearns's and Ayres's proxies in case they were unable to attend sessions. In conference each house casts one vote, and thus Griffin was always assured of a majority because Barden and Landrum always voted with the Republicans, making the split vote of five to two. The

Senate appointed its members of the Subcommittee on Labor. The number was again four Democrats—Kennedy,
Morse, McNamara, and Randolph—and three Republicans—Dirksen, Goldwater, and Prouty. Although the
Democrats controlled the Senate vote, the conservative
coalition had strong spokesmen in Dirksen and Goldwater.
Prouty also played an important part in the conference.[24]
With each side controlling the vote in one house, this
could have led to stalemate. But the Democratic leadership
had a big stake in getting a good labor bill passed. Otherwise Republicans could point out that labor bosses controlled the Democratic majority in Congress and prevented
passage of a reform bill. It also would reflect poorly on
Kennedy's leadership ability.

The lopsided vote in the House on Landrum-Griffin finally got the attention of the AFL-CIO leadership. After
the elections of 1958, labor leaders had thought they were
invulnerable. Now they realized they must try to salvage
what they could. Union leaders believed they had been betrayed by the House Democratic leadership; many thought
that Lyndon Johnson had done them in. After the House
vote the electrical workers union sent a letter to the 229
congressmen who voted for the Landrum-Griffin bill prom-
ising that the union would do everything in its power to
prove to laborers in each of their districts that the congressmen had voted against them and they should take appropriate action at the ballot box.[25]

Labor leaders came into the possession of a routine letter Lyndon Johnson sent on 15 August in response to the
flood of mail he received insisting that he vote for strong
labor legislation. His form letter called attention to his
vote for the Taft-Hartley Act in 1947 and to override Truman's veto and ended with the pledge that he was for "a
strong effective labor bill and I will vote that way every
chance I get." Some union leaders interpreted this to mean
that he supported the Landrum-Griffin bill. George Reedy
talked to Cy Anderson of the Railway Labor Executive As-

sociation. Anderson's advice was "to do nothing" about
the letter. Labor realized that what Johnson did was more
important than a letter he sent "to get anti-labor people off
your back." Reedy also explained the letter to Joe Miller of
the AFL-CIO Industrial Union Department, and he thought
that it would be "understood." James Carey of the electrical workers union defended Johnson at a meeting when
union men attacked his letter. Reedy also reported that
George Weaver of the electrical workers union understood
the reason for Johnson's letter and "was also impressed by
the fact that you advised labor against the strategy that led
to Landrum-Griffin."[26] Undoubtedly, the first reaction of
labor leaders was to strike out at the Democratic leadership, rather than to accept any blame themselves in their
frustration over losing a battle in a Congress so overwhelmingly Democratic.

At the first conference committee meeting in the Foreign Relations Room in the Capitol both sides agreed that
they could have their staffs present. Senator Kennedy had
Archibald Cox, and Goldwater had Michael Bernstein.
Griffin had his counsel, Kenneth McGuiness, and Charles
Ryan was available for Graham Barden. In addition, Lyndon Johnson and Everett Dirksen were influential behind
the scenes. Two or three days before the conference began,
John Kennedy and Carroll Kearns, who got along well, set
up a liaison meeting with Cox and McGuiness over break-
fast. During the conferences McGuiness had Cox to his
house for dinner several times, and many differences between the two sides were resolved during these informal
meetings.[27] When the question of chairmanship came up,
Barden deferred to Kennedy so he presided and Griffin was
the cochairman. Both sides agreed that all language that
was the same in both bills would not be changed.

The second and later meetings took place in the Old Supreme Court Chamber in the middle of the Capitol. The
conferees agreed that no specific information would be
given to the press but that, when appropriate, the chair-

man and cochairman would release statements. As the meetings progressed, the conservative coalition noticed that although Kennedy was not winning the key votes, the media and the public thought he was dominating the conference because information about the sessions came from him. Thus, during the second week both Griffin and Goldwater began making statements to the press about the committee's work.[28]

Title I was disposed of easily because the language was the same in each bill. The next title stimulated much discussion even though the two bills were not very far apart. The Senate bill exempted small unions from reporting. Landrum-Griffin did not so the Senate receded, as did the Senate conferees on the conflict-of-interest provision. The tougher Senate language on publishing the contents of reports was accepted seven to zero by the Senate conferees and three to three by the House. Thompson arrived late and made the vote four to three for the Senate version. At this second session the House receded once, the Senate eleven times, but none of the issues were terribly important except the small union exemption. The conferees then moved rapidly through the first six titles with Cox playing an important role as consultant. During one session Landrum blew up at the professor and later reported to Senator Richard Russell of Georgia that Cox had "been virtually a conferee" and the conservative coalition was "just about worn out" with him.[29]

Title VII, the Taft-Hartley amendments, stimulated the most discussion and created the greatest problems because the two bills were so far apart on important issues, especially no-man's land, picketing, and secondary boycotts. The no-man's land question was discussed first. The conference defeated proposed compromises by Prouty, Dirksen, and Perkins. The committee discussed the issues of building trades and economic strikers and, again, could not resolve the differences. Kennedy then asked for adjournment so he could prepare compromises. His proposals were rejected by the House conferees. In the afternoon session of 25 August, Dirksen asked that the room be cleared of everyone but members of the House and Senate. The conferees then discussed the time problem and their responsibility to their colleagues. Apparently this failed to break the impasse, so Dirksen announced that the minority would take the issues of organizational picketing and secondary boycotts to the floor of the Senate for instructions. Kennedy then announced that he would ask the Senate for instructions on the issues of no-man's land, common situs picketing, picketing of employers selling goods produced in a struck plant, and picketing sweatshops.

The following Monday, however, the Senate did not discuss the requests for instructions, and negotiations continued. Neither side wanted to debate the issues again, especially sweatshops, on the Senate floor. During this period, each morning Smith, Barden, Halleck, Landrum, Griffin, and McCabe met in Halleck's office to plan strategy and discuss tactics for the day. The Republicans apparently began counting heads and decided they did not have enough votes, and Dirksen got busy. *Newsweek* reported that Halleck's strategy was to support the southern Democrats and the "no compromise" issue and then blame the "won't do" Democratic Congress for not passing a labor bill and use it as a political issue in the elections of 1960. But Dirksen wanted to avoid another fight on the Senate floor so he pushed for compromise. Also of importance, at this point Richard Grey of the building and construction trades of the AFL-CIO sent a telegram asking James Mitchell what the administration's position was on the Denver building trades doctrine. Mitchell responded that the administration had declared on numerous occasions that the doctrine should be reversed.[30]

At the 1 September meeting the deadlock seemed to break loose. Kennedy proposed a number of compromises: exempt the clothing industry from the secondary boycott restrictions; overturn the Denver building trades doctrine;

legalize publicity to consumers without picketing; and make an unfair labor practice by the employer a defense for union organizational picketing. The conservative coalition then presented its counterproposals: exempt the garment workers; accept Kennedy's publicity proposal; permit organizational picketing if the employer illegally recognized the current union or made a "sweetheart" contract; and drop the common situs picketing issue because it was not in either bill.[31]

The give and take then began. Griffin offered to accept modified language to permit boycotting of garment sweatshops. In return, the House would recede on its provision allowing an employer to file suit for damages resulting from organizational picketing. This was accepted, and the provision for consumer picketing was retained. Kennedy then urged the conferees to come to an agreement on common situs picketing, which provoked extensive discussion. Barden stated that House rules prohibited acceptance of anything that was not in the original House bills. Thompson responded that he had asked the House parliamentarian and was given the "horseback" opinion that this issue would be germane and could be discussed. Kennedy also argued that they were writing entirely new language on hot cargo and secondary boycotts, which Barden supported. When Barden remained adamant on the point, Kennedy said he would take the issue of common situs picketing to the Senate floor if necessary. That afternoon, though, several of the conferees, including Landrum, Dirksen, and also Lyndon Johnson, asked the House parliamentarian about the germane issue, and he then reversed himself and said that overturning the Denver doctrine would be out of order.[32]

On 2 September a majority of the conferees agreed on all outstanding questions except common situs. When they discussed exempting building trade unions in the secondary boycott section, the point of order question surfaced again. Wayne Morse wanted to raise the issue in the Senate to get a decision, and Frank Thompson suggested trying to get the House to vote to overrule the parliamentarian. Kennedy then questioned the garment industry exemption, which was a parallel issue, and Landrum and Griffin said they would oppose raising the point of order.

The impasse was resolved when the Democratic leadership decided to abandon the building trades on common situs picketing. As George Reedy pointed out to Lyndon Johnson, those unions had been consistently Republican so why should the Democrats "go to bat" for them "simply because Mitchell wrote a letter to Dick Grey to pay off past favors." Besides, he noted, Title VII was in the bill primarily because the building trades wanted sweeteners to begin with, and this gave the Republicans an excuse to add other Taft-Hartley amendments. "Without that excuse, the Kennedy-Ervin bill would have gone sailing through both houses of Congress," he added, "and both the Democrats and labor would be in much better shape" than they were with the Landrum-Griffin Act.[33]

During a recess Thompson discussed compromise language on the building trades issue, and Sam Rayburn and Lyndon Johnson agreed to support it. Kennedy then announced that he would temporarily abandon common situs and introduce the question as a separate bill later. He had the assurances of the Senate majority and minority leaders that they would schedule the bill the next year. That afternoon, at a last session in the Old Supreme Court Chamber, the conferees agreed on the final language of the last remaining issues. Senator Morse and Representative Perkins announced that they would not support the conference report. On 3 September the Senate voted ninety-five to two to accept the report (Morse and Langer of North Dakota held out). On 4 September the House voted 353 to 52 to accept it, and Eisenhower signed the Landrum-Griffin Act into law on 14 September 1959. When asked what name it should carry, Kennedy suggested "The Labor-Management Reform Act." It became the Labor-Management Reporting and Disclosure Act of 1959.[34]

Phil Landrum and Robert Griffin were quoted in the *New York Times* as saying, "We don't feel we have compromised on any principles." The Landrum-Griffin Act made the following changes in the Taft-Hartley Act:

1. Prohibited all secondary boycotts, including hot cargo, except on farmed-out work that is being struck.[35]
2. Prohibited representational picketing unless a petition for election is filed within thirty days.
3. Gave states no-man's-land jurisdiction over cases the NLRB had not assumed jurisdiction over, as of 31 August 1959.
4. Permitted economic strikers to vote within twelve months of the beginning of the strike.
5. Allowed prehire agreements and a union shop seven days after employment begins in the building trades and maritime unions.
6. Delegated authority to NLRB regional directors to conduct elections.
7. Removed the noncommunist affidavit requirement for union officials.
8. Permitted the president to appoint an acting general counsel for the NLRB.
9. Established the legality of restricting subcontracting in the garment industry.
10. Permitted publicizing nonunion goods to consumers.
11. Prohibited employers from making (a) expenditures to prevent unionization or for spying on employees, (b) payments to union officials or employees, (c) payments to employees to induce them to influence other employees.[36]

A Bureau of the Budget memorandum to President Eisenhower noted that he had supported the bill of rights and thus the Landrum-Griffin Act gave him everything he had asked for in labor legislation except the bonuses he had not requested: a hot cargo provision, secondary boycotts not extended to the garment industry, no requirement to bar-

gain during the life of a contract, and no requirement that
the NLRB be bipartisan. The memo also noted, erro-
neously, that although the noncommunist affidavit requirement was lifted, the law did not ban communists
from being union officials, but "this difference does not appear to be significant." Eisenhower had received almost all
he had asked for, plus some additional items like hot cargo,
and in almost the exact language the administration had
requested.[37]

Wayne Morse was outraged at what he considered to be
John Kennedy's betrayal of unions. After the final vote, he
wrote Walter Reuther that he could not understand why
the UAW was heaping "high political praise" on the Massachusetts senator when Kennedy had betrayed the union
on the "anti-labor bill." On five questions—no-man's-land,
bonding, consumer picketing, struck goods agreements,
and inspection of membership lists—Morse had moved
that the Senate conferees stand in disagreement and take
the disputes to the Senate for instructions. He was convinced that he could have prevailed in the Senate on "several of these issues and the final bill would have been
much better than the vicious Kennedy-Landrum-Griffin
bill" that passed. But in each case, Morse lamented, "Kennedy voted with the Republicans and prevented further
Senate consideration." Morse was at "a complete loss to
understand how any labor leader can sanction the phoni-
ness of Kennedy's so-called liberalism."[38]

Organized labor got exactly what it said it did not
want—a tough labor law. The AFL-CIO tried to pin the label "killer bill" on it as Taft-Hartley had been called the
"slave labor law" twelve years earlier. Nevertheless, the
union got many items it wanted. As George Reedy recalled, "they did some hollering," but they were "so
damned happy" to get the prehire provisions and modifications of the secondary boycott. Of course, if organized labor had not demanded sweeteners and thus opened up
Taft-Hartley to other amendments, or if the leaders had

strongly supported the Kennedy-Ervin bill in the Senate as Johnson recommended or the Elliott bill in the House of Representative, perhaps they would not have gotten such a tough law as the Landrum-Griffin Act.[39] They should have accepted Kennedy's two-bill approach or listened when the House leadership told them what legislation was possible in 1959.

The real winners, of course, were management, the conservative coalition, Dwight D. Eisenhower, and the effective staff with which he had surrounded himself.

8. The Impact of the Law

Evidence of the impact of Landrum-Griffin on labor-management relations is scarce, often biased, frequently contradictory, and inconclusive. Some observations can be made, however, on the basis of a few years' experience with the operation of the law.

For the first time in American history a federal agency was charged with refereeing the internal operation of private organizations. To accomplish its new supervisory role in labor-management relations, the Department of Labor established a Bureau of Labor Management Reports. After 1963 the day-to-day administration of the policy was handled by the Office of Labor Management Standards Enforcement, headed by an assistant secretary of labor. In addition, the Department of Labor established six regional offices, twenty-four area offices, and twenty resident compliance offices. Personnel in these offices administer the Landrum-Griffin Act, the Employee Retirement Income Security Act, and the Veterans' Reemployment Rights Program. They also cooperate in the President's Anti–Organized Crime Program.[1]

Title I, the bill of rights, appears to have had the greatest impact on rank-and-file union members. The language in this section is very ambiguous as a result of political compromise and especially the way this title was written on the Senate floor. The title of the law was intended to guarantee democracy in unions, and when dissident members found they could obtain redress under the new law, they became more outspoken and assertive. During the first decade of the law's operation, more than 8,000 private legal actions were taken under Title I, compared to about 850 civil and criminal actions under Titles II through VI. The courts have been quite liberal in interpreting the rights of union members. *Salzhandler* v. *Caputo* (316 F 2d 445, 2d Circuit, certiorari denied by the Supreme Court in 1965, 375 U.S. 946) is the principal decision interpreting Title I. In that case the court held that for a member to libel a union officer is permissible and an unpunishable exercise of free speech. But Title I does not require unions to admit any person to membership and, as a result, racial and other forms of discrimination still exist in labor unions.[2] And, of course, it is weak in not providing financial assistance to aggrieved union members who wish to bring suit to maintain their rights.

Titles II and V, requiring financial reporting and fiduciary responsibilities of union officers and those handling union funds, have had a significant financial impact on unions. The bonding requirements have placed a heavy financial burden on unions, as have the high mailing costs for election notices, and the reporting requirements have forced unions to add numerous lawyers and bookkeepers to their staffs. This has been particularly burdensome for small locals and has resulted in a significant number of mergers and in raising membership dues to accommodate the additional expenses. But Title II has had "the desirable impact of making unions more dutiful in maintaining accurate and complete records, particularly of financial transactions." Often members suspect that their union has financial problems and can confirm their suspicions by checking the Title II reports. Yet the Department of Labor policy is to accept these reports without question unless a specific union is being investigated. The result is that inaccurate reports are accepted and no check is made to ascertain that reports are even being filed. For example, the Department of Labor did not notice that the United Mine Workers were not keeping Title II records until an investigation of a fraudulent election was undertaken. There are no meaningful enforcement sanctions for Title II. As for the effectiveness of Title V provisions outlawing embezzlement and misuse of union funds, criminal activity in labor organizations is about as pervasive now as it was when Landrum-Griffin was enacted. In 1978 a Senate committee again investigated corruption in unions and a deputy attorney general testified before that committee that three hundred local unions, or one-half of 1 percent, were "severely influenced by racketeers" and "major racketeering problems" could be found in five or six international unions.[3] Conditions had changed very little since the McClellan Committee hearing two decades earlier: racketeering still existed but only in a small percentage of the nation's unions.

Title III controlled the rights of unions to place locals under trusteeship. Here again, as with racketeering, the problem resided in only a few unions, but where it existed, the McClellan Committee revealed, the locals were sometimes unmercifully exploited. A study in 1979 revealed that there were 303 trusteeships compared with 492 in 1959. More important, in 1959 there were 288 trusteeships of over eighteen months' duration, the maximum allowed by Landrum-Griffin, and in 1975 this number was down to 85. In addition, as a result of the law, many unions revised their constitutions to provide detailed specifications for the purposes and procedures for imposing trusteeships. Again, as with the problem of reporting, the Department of Labor was faulted for inadequate supervision. From 1959 to 1971 the secretary of labor initiated only four lawsuits under Title III, "which . . . indicates a serious lack of diligence." In one of these cases, involving the UMW, it took seven years to get the trusteeship declared invalid. This experience did not encourage other union members to seek the assistance of the secretary of labor in trusteeship situations.[4]

The purpose of Title IV was to ensure greater democracy in union elections. The law empowered the secretary of labor to act on behalf of union members in allegations of impropriety in elections. But the Department of Labor must also represent the public interest; therefore sometimes it is forced to play conflicting roles. When this happens, according to one source, the department has "consistently favored the public interest over the rights of the member complainant." The department would not file suit if it was determined that the election result was not affected by violations and, most important, it was department policy not to investigate until after the election results were known. In the latter case often the investigation came too late because evidence had disappeared or the rerun election was held too late to afford the complainant effective relief. As one source has imaginatively put it, Title IV has become "a buffalo gun in an area generally troubled with mice."[5] The case of the United Mine Workers and Joseph "Jock" Yablonski illustrates this problem vividly.

When John L. Lewis decided to retire, his hand-picked successor, Tony Boyle, easily won the UMW presidency. Boyle proceeded to entrench his position by increasing pensions 33 percent, thus ensuring support from the numerous pensioners, and in a short time allegations of misconduct and malfeasance in office were rampant in the coal mining country. No one had seriously challenged a UMW president since 1926, when Lewis successfully turned back an effort to unseat him. But in 1969 Jock Yablonski ran a hard-hitting campaign for president against Boyle on the platform of his supporters, Miners for Democracy, to oust Boyle and clean up corruption in the UMW. Six months before the election, counsel Joseph Rauh, representing the Miners for Democracy, repeatedly asked Secretary of Labor George Schultz to investigate campaign irregularities and gave details of more than a thousand violations of the law. Schultz responded that his department's policy was not to investigate until the election was over. After a vicious campaign, on 9 December 1969 Boyle decisively defeated Yablonski, overwhelmingly in those precincts where the latter did not have poll watchers. Some three weeks after the election Yablonski, his wife, and his daughter were found murdered in their beds in their home in Clarksville, Pennsylvania. Charges were later brought against three men and a woman, alleging that the Yablonskis were murdered to prevent Jock from testifying before a federal grand jury about UMW campaign irregularities, the filing of false or no financial reports, and the millions of dollars of UMW funds unaccounted for.

As a result of widespread media coverage of the murders and subsequent publicity, Secretary Schultz eventually ordered an investigation of the election in March 1970. The trial date was set for September 1971. By that time, of course, vital evidence such as the original ballots and tally sheets had disappeared.[6] The investigation came too late to help the Yablonski family.

Title VI contains miscellaneous provisions on extortionate picketing, retention of rights under state and federal laws, criminal contempt, separability, and similar items.

Robert P. Griffin observed that "to provide guarantees of democracy within the union while maintaining the effectiveness of the union as an institution," which was the purpose of the Landrum-Griffin Act, "is not an easy task."[7] The evidence of success here is conflicting and contradictory.

One study reported that employers, who supported the Landrum-Griffin bill in hopes of breaking the power of omnipotent labor leaders over their members, were subsequently complaining of too much democracy. Rank-and-file members were acting unreasonably in rejecting contracts, for example, and labor leaders were "afraid to stand up to them for fear that, if they do they will lose the next election." Some employers could no longer depend on union officials to be persuasive and were soon yearning for the "bad old days" when they negotiated contracts with autocratic bosses. Certainly democratic organizations are more difficult for management to negotiate with in the short run.[8]

This democratization, the same source reported, had resulted in changed relationships between some parent unions and their affiliates. Before 1959 some parent union officials dealt autocratically with their locals and now must be more responsive to local challenges to authority. They must also try to negotiate a tougher bargain or face rejection of contracts by members. The balance has also shifted the other way in some cases, and local officials are now quick to seek advice and guidance from the parent union. In some instances the local officials are so responsive to their members that they were described as "paranoid—afraid to move."[9]

Philip Taft pointed out that many union secretaries and business agents are very devoted to their union and are willing to perform their tasks for small remuneration or honor, and they are not trained bookkeepers. Thus apparent embezzlement of funds is often merely "poor or inexpert keeping of accounts." As a result of Landrum-Griffin requirements, "a fear of holding office" on the local level has "permeated the ranks" of some unions. Taft further noted that if the Landrum-Griffin Act had been in effect earlier it would have been much more difficult for the old CIO to deal with communism in its ranks after World War II.[10]

The first six titles of Landrum-Griffin have certainly not achieved the objective of cleaning up the primary target of the McClellan Committee, the teamsters. In the 1980s more than one hundred teamster leaders were indicted or convicted of breaking laws. In 1978 it was reported that the Department of Justice intended to use the Racketeer Influenced and Corrupt Organizations Act of 1970 to replace teamster leaders with court-appointed trustees. Three of the last five teamster presidents received criminal convictions while in office; a presidential commission reported in

1986 that a fourth president had allowed organized crime to siphon off pension funds, and the fifth, Jackie Presser, was scheduled to go on trial for paying $700,000 to mob-related "ghost employees" who did no work for the union. (Presser died 9 July 1988 while under indictment).[11]

Finally, Title VII, the most controversial section of the law, has had a significant impact on labor-management relations although, again, not necessarily on the unions whose nefarious activities were exposed by the Rackets Committee. First, it has impeded the growth of certain unions. Those that used organizational picketing as a weapon have had their activities severely restricted. Unions organizing retail employees, though, have been curtailed only slightly. The bans on hot cargo agreements and secondary consumer picketing have hurt the teamsters and the lithographers but have not affected the garment and building trade unions because they are exempt from the restrictions. If the hot cargo ban had come earlier, it would have hurt the teamsters even more. But by 1959 Hoffa was firmly in control and the teamsters were able to use other legal leverage techniques in their negotiations. These proscriptions injure small unionized employers more than large corporations and give nonunionized companies "added strength to remain ununionized." These restrictions have, in turn, adversely affected union bargaining power.[12]

Second, these changes have helped management by giving open-shop employers further protection against organizational efforts (in addition to the bans on organizational picketing and secondary boycotts, permitting states to assume jurisdiction in no-man's land subjects union organizing efforts to codes that generally are more restrictive than federal law). They protect "neutral" employers from involvement in labor disputes through the ban on secondary boycotts and hot cargo agreements. Finally, the union employer's hand is strengthened in collective bargaining, especially by the ban on secondary boycotts.[13]

Third, by giving states jurisdiction over no-man's land, "unions and employers in a number of states are now permitted to engage in practices . . . not tolerated by the federal law." In those states the progress of labor-management relations was turned back a quarter of a century.[14]

Fourth, exempting the garment and building trades unions brought the law into conformity with the realities of existing conditions. But if it is useful to exempt these two industries from the ban on secondary boycotts and hot cargo agreements, the question arises as to whether these practices might serve a good purpose for other unions such as the lithographers.[15]

Fifth, partially restoring the franchise to economic strikers makes it more difficult for employers to obtain decertification of a striking union. Yet this change will not affect employers in labor surplus areas as much as it could in those with labor shortages.[16]

Finally, Title VII resolved the problem of delays in settling representational election cases by allowing the NLRB to delegate authority to regional directors. Unfortunately, Congress did not allow similar authority over delays in settling unfair labor practices cases. As an NLRB member noted, "Justice delayed is all too often justice denied."[17]

9. Some Assessments

The Republican government of the 1950s was oriented toward business, yet the Eisenhower years were also good in many ways for organized labor. In addition to union achievements such as the guaranteed annual wage and the merger of the AFL-CIO, other labor goals were reached during the decade. The minimum wage was increased, and, as George Meany recalled, "labor certainly made tremendous progress in health, education, medical care and things like that. . . . So the Eisenhower Administration, in my book, was by no means a bad time for labor."[1]

In 1953 Eisenhower and Taft tried an accommodationist approach to labor policy and sought common agreement on changes that experience with the Taft-Hartley Act had shown were needed. This approach was in keeping with Eisenhower's philosophy of incorporating unions into the corporate commonwealth state and also might attract labor support to the Republican party. But after Taft's premature death the party's conservative wing captured control of Congress and Eisenhower increasingly found his accommodationist policy unfeasible. As misuse of union funds and other union corruption were revealed late in his administration, the president exploited the resulting public indignation to persuade Congress to enact a tough labor reform bill to curb abuses by union officials and to force unions to follow democratic procedures. The resulting change in labor-management policy reflected the trend since 1932 of an increasing growth of bureaucracy and intrusion of the national government into affairs previously the realm of the states. This was achieved by Republicans who had been complaining about this trend when Democrats occupied the White House.

Public opinion proved to be the most important influence forcing congressional action on labor reform legislation. The rackets committee revelations informed private citizens of the need for reform. President Eisenhower's "nonpartisan" appeal for support for a specific "bipartisan" bill provided the catalyst for action. The subsequent public response to congressmen was particularly important to those freshmen who had never voted on labor bills and were undecided how to vote on a complex labor reform law.

The McClellan Committee hearings from 1957 to 1960 revealed that organized crime had penetrated the labor movement, and though corruption affected only a very small percentage of unions, it was pervasive and sinister where it existed. Most important, television brought the hearings into the homes of millions of Americans, and the public's attention focused on one man—Jimmy Hoffa—who appeared arrogant in using his vast powers and greedy in exploiting his numerous supporters. The hearings set the scene for Congress to pass legislation to curb labor bosses' power and union racketeering, just as the public mood had demanded that the "irresponsible" union leaders be controlled twelve years previously.

The presidential ambition of several senators at the end of the decade also influenced the outcome of labor reform legislation. By the same token, the course of the legislation through Congress greatly affected the careers of these politicians. Young John Kennedy established a good rapport with union leaders in trying to protect their interests and emerged from the battle with his reputation as a leader greatly enhanced. This experience undoubtedly promoted his candidacy for the presidency in 1960. Barry Goldwater likewise significantly improved his standing with his constituency, which assisted his efforts to gain the Republican presidential nomination in 1964. Lyndon Johnson's role as

Senate majority leader during the fight over labor legislation contributed to his evolving from a sectional leader to
one of national stature and allowed labor leaders to become
better acquainted with him, which became very important
when he became president in 1963.

The congressional elections of 1958 gave the Democrats
more control over Congress than they had had since the
New Deal. These gains were attributed largely to the successful efforts of labor—the party's largest and most powerful constituency—and labor leaders became overly
confident of their invulnerability. They misread this vote
just as they had in Truman's upset election in 1948. Management groups deliberately contributed to the idea that labor was invincible by a propaganda campaign that
convinced union leaders and the public that the Eighty-
sixth Congress would not pass legislation inimical to the
interests of organized labor.

Both labor and management forcefully lobbied Congress,
but the management groups were more cohesive in their
efforts and thus more effective ultimately than the labor
unions, which were seriously divided over goals and
strategy. The White House staff performed skillfully in co-
ordinating management lobbying for the bill. Business representatives had more success in mobilizing local pressure
on individual wavering congressmen than did labor lobbyists. But it was President Eisenhower's television appeal
that energized public opinion for one particular labor reform bill.

Because of this struggle and other current events, the
foreign press and even the American media began talking
about the "new" Eisenhower and his effective leadership.
They did not understand that the "hidden-hand" president,
as Fred I. Greenstein has labeled him, had displayed, un-
obtrusively, great leadership qualities throughout his presidency. Though he had six years of experience in dealing
with Congress, Eisenhower faced two major obstacles with
his legislative program in his last two years in office. First,

he was a lame-duck president, and second, the Democrats had overwhelming control of the Eighty-sixth Congress. His new congressional leaders, Charles Halleck and Everett Dirksen, were more effective than their predecessors, and they were fortunate in courting the conservative coalition to support the president's vetoes. The economic recession of 1958 prompted Democrats to dust off New Deal legislation to promote economic growth in 1959 and 1960, and the embattled president steadfastly fought government intervention in the economy. This intense partisan warfare over economic policy precluded the hidden-hand president from exerting his leadership in promoting his conservative economics policies, although a number of events coalesced in 1959 to give him the labor policy he wanted.

Labor leaders were not only seriously divided over objectives and strategy, but, because of supreme overconfidence, they overplayed their hand. So certain were they of victory that they demanded that Taft-Hartley sweeteners be added to a labor reform bill. Thus Taft-Hartley was opened up for further amendments, and management representatives could rightfully insist on changes in labor policy that they had been wanting for a decade. The result was a much tougher bill than labor leaders would have received had they accepted Kennedy's "two-package" approach to labor legislation. By refusing any compromise, labor leaders failed to eliminate some of the provisions in the bill that they most disliked.

The Republicans, although holding only a bare one-third of the congressional seats, were in a good political position to enact labor reform legislation. They obviously could not satisfy both labor and management, so they supported their primary constituency, big business, as usual. With the public outrage over union racketeering and corruption and Eisenhower's superb leadership, the Republicans were in the enviable position of either ending up with a tough bill or being able to blame the Democrats for getting no bill at all. The Democratic leaders, of course, saw clearly that, for political reasons, they could not accept the blame for preventing passage of a labor reform bill before the elections of 1960.

The Landrum-Griffin Act would not have passed Congress without the meshing of the conservative coalition. Many congressmen ignored the fact that corruption in organized labor came about because of the failure of the governments of states, counties, and cities. Southerners, strong supporters of states' rights, voted to expand significantly the power and regulatory force of the central government to confront racketeering. As one perceptive observer noted, the cities and states had all the necessary power to cope with corruption, but states'-rights advocates demanded federal action "to deal with crimes committed within the province of their own local police and legislatures."[2] Northern Republicans joined forces with those southerners to support a law that would retard unionization of the South and thus help maintain a pool of low-cost labor to attract new industry to the region.

Passage of the Landrum-Griffin Act demonstrated what happens when the committee system breaks down. It is highly unusual for Congress to approve legislation that has not been considered by the appropriate committee. Laws, especially complicated technical ones, should be written in committee after thorough investigation and careful deliberation. In this case, the bill was written under the glare of public scrutiny and in a politically charged atmosphere. The result, as with the Taft-Hartley Act, is a law with weaknesses that needed revision as soon as it was enacted. Based on his experience with passage of this legislation, Speaker Sam Rayburn decided, following the election of John Kennedy in 1960, that he must either "purge" or "pack" the Rules Committee for the new president's legislative program to have any chance of being considered by the House of Representatives.[3]

The Landrum-Griffin Act intruded the national government into the internal affairs of private organizations for the first time. One of the weaknesses in the law was to place the Department of Labor in charge of administering the new policy. This department often finds itself playing the conflicting roles of protecting either union members or public policy and must abandon one or the other. The problem is further compounded when the department adamantly pursues a policy of abrogation of responsibility. As one source noted, experience has "cast doubt upon the wisdom of placing responsibility for enforcing a statute against international union leadership in the Department of Labor."[4]

According to the minority counsel for the House Labor Committee, the act was further weakened because the conference report was hastily drafted and written by one person. As a result, judges trying to interpret the law sometimes had difficulty discerning congressional intent. This problem was particularly acute with respect to the Title VII provisions. The conference committee compromised by accepting the House-approved amendments to the Taft-Hartley Act with certain stipulations, but the conferees did not spell out their meanings or intent in regard to the provisos, leaving them for judges and administrators to interpret. Just as it took years to solve the legal issues surrounding the Taft-Hartley Act, so too with this new labor policy. Landrum-Griffin "spawned numerous controversies over its scope, its procedural guarantees, and its remedial provisions," but during the succeeding decade "a satisfactory resolution of most issues" was reached.[5]

Public opinion played a major role in the passage of the Wagner, Taft-Hartley, and Landrum-Griffin acts. Because the latter two placed restrictions on unions, they have other similarities.

Union leaders called the Taft-Hartley Act a slave labor law that would destroy the union movement. Similar predictions greeted the Landrum-Griffin Act as union spokesmen referred to it as a killer law. But, as one of the coauthors suggested, "If there are those who believed, or hoped, that the law would break the backs of legitimate unions, or impede the healthy growth of the great labor movement as a vital force in our economic system, I am pleased to report they will be disappointed."[6] Both laws have turned out to be good ones, and unions have had to learn to live with them.

Neither law has fulfilled the expectations of its authors. Each seemed to be directed at one labor leader who had received a bad press—John L. Lewis of the United Mine Workers in 1947 and Jimmy Hoffa of the teamsters in 1959. Finally, both laws contain provisions that were ill-considered and in need of revisions. But changes in the national labor policy do not come quickly or easily. The issue of common situs picketing, for example, is still unresolved, and glaring problems remain in labor policy. Perhaps as our industrial society continues to change rapidly with the approach of the twenty-first century, they will eventually be addressed.

Notes

Abbreviations

CR	*Congressional Record*
DDEL	Dwight D. Eisenhower Library
JFKL	John Fitzgerald Kennedy Library
LBJL	Lyndon Baines Johnson Library
NA	National Archives
PPPUS	Public Papers of the Presidents of the United States (Washington, D.C.: U.S. Government Printing Office)
RG	Record Group
SRL	Sam Rayburn Library
WPRL	Walter P. Reuther Library

Chapter 1. Unions and the Democrats

1. U.S. *Statutes at Large*, vol. 49, pt. 1, pp. 449-50.

2. James B. Atleson, *Values and Assumptions in American Labor Law* (Amherst: Univ. of Massachusetts Press, 1983), 19. Christopher L. Tomlins, *The State and the Unions* (London: Cambridge Univ. Press, 1985), 26n., observes that this was standard NLRB policy since 1936.

3. Harry A. Millis and Emily Clark Brown, *From the Wagner Act to Taft-Hartley* (Chicago: Univ. of Chicago Press, 1950), is the best study of the new labor policy.

4. Joel Seidman, *American Labor from Defense to Reconversion* (Chicago: Univ. of Chicago Press, 1953), is a good account of labor in World War II. See Gilbert J. Gall, *The Politics of Right to Work* (Westport, Ct.: Greenwood Press, 1988), 15-18, for maintenance of membership clauses during the war.

5. Tomlins, *The State and the Unions*, 252-53.

6. For the formation and growth of the conservative coalition, consult James T. Patterson, *Congressional Conservatism and the New Deal* (Lexington: Univ. of Kentucky Press, 1967), and Mack C. Shelley, II, *The Permanent Majority: The Conservative Coalition in*

the United States Congress (University: Univ. of Alabama Press, 1983).

7. For the enactment of this change in labor policy, see R. Alton Lee, *Truman and Taft-Hartley: A Question of Mandate* (Lexington: Univ. of Kentucky Press, 1966).

8. U.S. *Statutes at Large,* vol. 61, pt. 1, p. 137. Indeed, Taft argued that the purpose of his law was to restore the goals of the Wagner Act, which "had been distorted by its pro-union administrators."

9. Quoted in James A. Gross, *The Reshaping of the National Labor Relations Board* (Albany: State Univ. of New York Press, 1981), 259.

10. Howell John Harris, *The Right to Manage* (Madison: Univ. of Wisconsin Press, 1982), 157.

11. Richard Edwards, *Contested Terrain: The Transformation of the Workplace in the Twentieth Century* (New York: Basic Books, 1971), 203-4n.; Atleson, *Values and Assumptions in American Labor Law,* 147, 149.

12. William H. Miernyk, *Trade Unions in the Age of Affluence* (New York: Random House, 1962), 107-9; David Brody, *Workers in Industrial America* (New York: Oxford Univ. Press, 1980), 192.

13. Brody, *Workers,* 240-41.

14. Joseph A. Loftus, "LMRDA in Retrospect," in Ralph Slovenko, ed., *Symposium on the Labor-Management Reporting and Disclosure Act of 1959* (New Orleans: Tulane Univ., 1961), 9.

15. Edwards, *Contested Terrain,* 161.

16. Martin Halpern, "Taft-Hartley and the Defeat of the Progressive Alternative in the United Auto Workers," *Labor History* 27 (Spring 1986): 204-6; Brody, *Workers,* 227-28.

17. Ronald Radosh, *American Labor and United States Foreign Policy* (New York: Random House, 1969), 435-37.

18. Thomas W. Braden, "I'm Glad the CIA Is 'Immoral,' " *Saturday Evening Post* 240 (20 May 1967), 10-12. George Meany claimed in 1953 that the AFL had been active in Germany and other West European countries since 1946 and that his union also financed "literature that goes behind the Iron Curtain" (interview with George Meany in "What Labor Wants," *U.S. News and World Report* 35 [6 Nov. 1953]: 60).

19. Brody, *Workers,* 216, 232.

20. Lee, *Truman and Taft-Hartley,* chap. 7; Benjamin Aaron, "Amending the Taft-Hartley Act: A Decade of Frustration," *Industrial and Labor Relations Review* 11 (April 1958): 331-33.

21. Lee, *Truman and Taft-Hartley*, 221-30. Eisenhower's address to the AFL is in the *New York Times*, 18 Sept. 1952.

22. Gerald Pomper, "Labor Legislation: The Revision of Taft-Hartley in 1953-1954," *Labor History* 6 (Spring 1965): 146-47, 154-56.

Chapter 2. Unions and the Republicans

1. Ann C. Whitman Diary, 20 May 1960, DDEL. Elmo Richardson, *The Presidency of Dwight D. Eisenhower* (Lawrence: Regents Press of Kansas, 1979), 147, notes that Eisenhower had a "personal bias against labor leaders."

2. Robert Griffith, "Dwight D. Eisenhower and the Corporate Commonwealth," *American Historical Review* 87 (Feb. 1982): 88; Robert Keith Gray, *Eighteen Acres under Glass* (Garden City, N.Y.: Doubleday, 1962), 258. Donald R. Brand, *Corporatism and the Rule of Law* (Ithaca: Cornell Univ. Press, 1988), 288, states that the first New Deal sought to "transform trade associations and trade unions into institutions serving public rather than private interests." Eisenhower's philosophy was quite similar to this goal.

3. James T. Patterson, *Mr. Republican* (Boston: Houghton Mifflin, 1972), 583-85.

4. Dwight D. Eisenhower, *Mandate for Change* (Garden City, N.Y.: Doubleday, 1963), 90-91; Durkin quote in *Commonwealth* 59 (23 Oct. 1953): 58.

5. *PPPUS, 1953*, pp. 28-29; *Fortune* 47 (Jan. 1953): 63-66.

6. Eisenhower, *Mandate for Change*, 195-96; Bernard Shanley Diary, 616a, DDEL; Lee, *Truman and Taft-Hartley*, 63, 72.

7. Pomper, "Labor Legislation," 144-46; Shanley Diary, 909-10.

8. Walter P. Reuther to Sherman Adams, 5 May, 9 June 1953, GF 19N-1, Department of Labor Papers, DDEL. The "no more Bohlens" quote is from R. Alton Lee, *Dwight D. Eisenhower: Soldier and Statesman* (Chicago: Nelson-Hall, 1981), 201.

9. Pomper, "Labor Legislation," 147-48.

10. *Current Biography, 1954* (New York: H.H. Wilson Company, 1954), 647-49.

11. Shanley Diary, 624a, 1188a, 795.

12. Ibid., 924, 959, 1050, 1058-59.

13. Ibid., 1115-16.

14. Memorandum attached to letter from H.J. Spoerer to J.L. Mauthe, 27 Aug. 1953, OF 124-G, DDEL.

15. Herbert S. Parmet, *Eisenhower and the American Crusades* (New York: Macmillan, 1972), 328; Gary W. Reichard, *The Reaffir-*

mation of Republicanism: Eisenhower and the Eighty-Third Congress (Knoxville: Univ. of Tennessee Press, 1975), 144; Shanley Diary, 117.

16. Memorandum, Bernard Shanley and Gerald Morgan to the president, 30 Sept. 1953, Ann Whitman File, Administration Series, DDEL; Shanley Diary, 1120, 1136, 1140, 1153, 1188a, 1188b, 1207; *Newsweek* 42 (21 Sept. 1953): 28.

17. Eisenhower, *Mandate for Change,* 197-99.

18. Martin P. Durkin, "The Labor Program: Why I Resigned," *Vital Speeches* 20 (15 Oct. 1953): 6-8. Reichard, *Reaffirmation of Republicanism,* 144n., says Smith's correspondence with Senator Saltonstall at the time confirms Eisenhower's disclaimers that he made definite promises to Durkin.

19. Pomper, "Labor Legislation," 149; Reichard, *Reaffirmation of Republicanism,* 144.

20. George Meany, "What Labor Wants," *U.S. News & World Report* 35 (6 Nov. 1953): 57; Eisenhower, *Mandate for Change,* 291, 490.

21. *Current Biography, 1954,* 462-64.

22. *New York Times,* 20 Nov. 1953; *Vital Speeches* 20 (15 Oct. 1953): 12; *PPPUS, 1953,* 1106.

23. Shanley Diary, 1294-97. For Mitchell's opposition to a national right-to-work law, see Gall, *The Politics of Right to Work,* 98.

24. Staff Secretary, Cabinet Series, 15 Dec. 1953, DDEL.

25. *PPPUS, 1954,* 41-44; Memo, Bernard M. Shanley to the president, 30 Sept. 1953, Ann Whitman File, Administrative Series, DDEL. Organized labor was obsessed with repeal of section 14(b). The Johnson administration wanted to discuss with the Business Council and the Executive Committee of the AFL-CIO the idea of asking Congress for an additional $2 to 3 billion for education, health, and Social Security programs to stimulate the economy. The Johnson aide promoting this stimulant was "never . . . as disgusted in my life" as when the AFL-CIO wanted only to discuss repeal of 14(b), which they called the "slave labor act" (Hugh Gardner Ackley Oral History Interview, pp. 27-28, LBJL).

26. James C. Hagerty Diary, 12 Jan. 1953, DDEL.

27. *PPPUS, 1954,* p. 50. The "I'll confuse them" quote is from Lee, *Eisenhower,* 181.

28. Arthur J. Goldberg, "Analysis of Ike's Labor Message," Reuther Papers, Box 422, Folder 1, WPRL.

29. Pomper, "Labor Legislation," 152. Arthur Goldberg thought the proposals were "sugar coating to disguise new anti-labor restric-

tions" (Reuther Papers, Box 422, Folder 1, WPRL). Eisenhower reported to his cabinet that David McDonald of the United Steel Workers urged him not to push further for Taft-Hartley revision in 1954 because labor and management "were now in the middle of an unprecedented era of good feeling" and congressional debate on the act would dampen this feeling (Minnich Series, Labor Legislation, 9 April 1954, DDEL).

30. *Congressional Record*, 83d Cong., 2d sess, pp. 5827-29.

31. Ibid., 5840-43, 6202-3; Pomper, "Labor Legislation," 153-54; Hagerty Diary, 10 May 1954. Senator Smith was convinced at one point that Eisenhower did not "quite know what it [Goldwater's amendment] was all about!" See Reichard, *Reaffirmation of Republicanism*, 145-46; *Nation* 178 (22 May 1954): 443.

32. *PPPUS, 1955*, 26; *PPPUS, 1956*, 22; Aaron, "Amending the Taft-Hartley Act," 336-37.

33. John B. Rae, *The American Automobile* (Chicago: Univ. of Chicago Press, 1965), 210-11.

34. Archie Robinson, *George Meany and His Times* (New York: Simon and Schuster, 1981), 163; Arthur J. Goldberg, *AFL-CIO: Labor United* (New York: McGraw-Hill, 1956), chap. 5, esp. 102. Unfortunately, as Robert Zeiger has pointed out in "Toward a History of the CIO," *Labor History* 26 (Fall 1985): 514-15, there is no substantial history of the merger and we have to rely on Goldberg's account, which was put together by the CIO legal staff.

35. Frank W. McCulloch and Tim Bornstein, *The National Labor Relations Board* (New York: Praeger, 1974), 61.

36. Seymour Scher, "Congressional Committee Members as Independent Agency Overseers: A Case Study," *American Political Science Review* 54 (Dec. 1960): 911-20; Seymour Scher, "Regulatory Agency Control through Appointment: The Case of the Eisenhower Administration and the NLRB," *Journal of Politics* 23 (Nov. 1961): 667-88. See also William N. Cooke and Frederick H. Gautschi III, "Political Bias in NLRB Unfair Labor Practices Decisions," *Industrial and Labor Relations Review* 35 (July 1982): 539-40.

37. James P. Mitchell, "Where I Stand: Decent Wages and Working Conditions for All," *Vital Speeches* 20 (25 Dec. 1953): 130; Cabinet meeting, 28 Oct. 1955, Minnich Series, Labor Legislation, DDEL; Legislative Conferences, 12 Dec. 1955 and 4 Dec. 1957, ibid.; Malcolm Moos, "The Election of 1956," in Arthur M. Schlesinger, Jr., and Fred L. Israel, eds., *History of American Presidential Elections*, 6 vols. (New York: Chelsea House, 1971), 4:3350; Robinson, *George Meany*, 208n.

Chapter 3. Enter Mr. Beck . . . and Mr. Hoffa

1. Statement addressed to White House Aide Charles F. Willis, 29 Oct. 1953, GF 126-K, Taft-Hartley, Eisenhower Papers, DDEL.

2. William Howard Moore, *The Kefauver Committee and the Politics of Crime, 1950-1952* (Columbia: Univ. of Missouri Press, 1974), chap. 7.

3. Robert F. Kennedy, *The Enemy Within* (New York: Popular Library, 1960), 205; Robinson, *George Meany*, 186.

4. Meany, "What Labor Wants," 58-59.

5. Donald Edwin Walker, "The Congressional Career of Clare E. Hoffman (Ph.D. dissertation: Michigan State Univ., 1982), 34-46, 49-50, 175, 317.

6. Clark R. Mollenhoff, *Tentacles of Power* (Cleveland: World, 1965), 7, 37, 50; the Ratner quote is from *New York Times*, 14 Aug. 1958.

7. Mollenhoff, *Tentacles of Power*, 77, 81, 91-92. Edward Mc-Cabe thought Bellino played a very important role in these investigations, not only because of his ability but also because he had contact with other former FBI agents. McCabe had known Bellino when he was an investigator for the Government Operations Committee during and after World War II, and he persuaded McConnell to hire him (interview with Edward A. McCabe, 11 May 1987, hereafter cited as McCabe interview).

8. Mollenhoff, *Tentacles of Power*, 8.

9. Milton MacKaye, "The Senate's New Investigator," *Saturday Evening Post* 228 (13 Aug. 1955): 67.

10. Mollenhoff, *Tentacles of Power*, 124; Kennedy, *Enemy Within*, 20.

11. Mollenhoff, *Tentacles of Power*, 22; Arthur M. Schlesinger, Jr., *Robert Kennedy and His Times* (New York: Ballantine Books, 1978), 151-53; Walter Sheridan, *The Rise and Fall of Jimmy Hoffa* (New York: Saturday Review Press, 1972), 30-31.

12. Kennedy, *Enemy Within*, 30-31.

13. Schlesinger, *Kennedy*, 153. Determining committee membership posed problems. In addition to McClellan, Government Operations was composed of Henry "Scoop" Jackson, Democrat from Washington, and Stuart Symington, Democrat from Missouri, both considered prolabor, and antilabor Sam Ervin, North Carolina Democrat, Karl Mundt, Republican from South Dakota, Chapman Revercomb, Republican from West Virginia, and Joseph McCarthy. Kennedy's Committee on Labor and Public Welfare included Demo-

crats Matthew Neely from West Virginia, Patrick McNamara from Michigan, and Wayne Morse from Oregon, and Irving Ives, Republican from New York, all considered prolabor, and two antilabor senators, William Purtell, Republican from Connecticut, and Barry Goldwater, Republican from Arizona. The Republicans had no trouble serving on the special committee, for the teamsters union and its president were strongly supportive of their party. It was easily agreed that Ives would serve as vice-chairman and McCarthy, Goldwater, and Mundt wanted to serve on the committee. Such service presented some difficulties for Democrats. Jackson declined because of teamster power in Washington; his service would be considered an antiunion effort, and he was coming up for reelection in 1958. Symington also declined because of his friendship with Harold Gibbons of St. Louis, one of Hoffa's top aides in the Central Conference of Teamsters.

14. Quote from ibid., 154; see also Herbert S. Parmet, *Jack: The Struggles of John F. Kennedy* (New York: Dial, 1980), 417.

15. John L. McClellan, *Crime without Punishment* (New York: Duell, Sloan and Pearce, 1962), 208-9.

16. Mollenhoff, *Tentacles of Power*, 141, 151; Schlesinger, *Kennedy*, 158-59. Hoffa was incredibly casual in handling teamster funds. In the early 1960s, when James Reynolds of the Department of Labor was administering the Landrum-Griffin bonding requirements, the teamster officials' bonding lapsed. Hoffa walked into Reynolds's office and said, "Suppose I put a cigar box on that desk of yours in a half an hour with a half million dollars cash in it. Would you consider that my bond?" "Where are you going to get the money [for bond to guarantee your officials will not steal union money]," Reynolds demanded. "From the treasury," Hoffa replied (James Reynolds Oral History Interview, p. 20, JFKL).

17. Meany quote in Robinson, *George Meany*, 196; Sheridan, *Rise and Fall of Jimmy Hoffa*, 18.

18. Sheridan, *Rise and Fall of Jimmy Hoffa*, 93-97.

19. McClellan, *Crime without Punishment*, 83-88.

20. John Bartlow Martin, "The Making of a Labor Boss," *Saturday Evening Post* 232 (18 July 1959): 103.

21. The story of this Hoffa trial can be pieced together from a number of sources from which the information in the following paragraphs is taken: Mollenhoff, *Tentacles of Power*, 147, 154-55, 186-89, 198-99, 206-7; Sheridan, *Rise and Fall of Jimmy Hoffa*, 25-36; McClellan, *Crime without Punishment*, 22-24; Kennedy, *Enemy Within*, 61-67.

22. John Bartlow Martin, "Hoffa Takes the Stand," *Saturday Evening Post* 232 (4 July 1959): 27.

23. Quoted in Schlesinger, *Kennedy*, 168.

24. Ibid., 169; Sheridan, *Rise and Fall of Jimmy Hoffa*, 128-29.

25. Mollenhoff, *Tentacles of Power*, 221-22.

26. Robinson, *George Meany*, 192-202. Reuther notified Meany in March 1958 that his UAW had approved the Ethical Practices Code (Reuther to Meany, 7 March 1958, Reuther Papers, Box 301, Folder 6, WPRL).

27. Kennedy, *Enemy Within*, 183-88; Stuart Bruce Kaufman, *A Vision of Unity* (Urbana: Univ. of Illinois Press, 1987), 139-40, 145.

28. Kaufman, *Vision of Unity*, 188-205.

29. Ibid., 220-27.

30. Daniel Bell, "Nate Shefferman, Union Buster," *Fortune* 57 (Feb. 1958): 120, 209; John Hutchinson, *The Imperfect Union* (New York: Dutton, 1970), 179-82.

31. Sheridan, *Rise and Fall of Jimmy Hoffa*, 31-33, 49-51; Mollenhoff, *Tentacles of Power*, 233-35; Kennedy, *Enemy Within*, 206-15; Hutchinson, *Imperfect Union*, 170-74.

32. Victor C. Reuther, *The Brothers Reuther* (Boston: Houghton Mifflin, 1976), chap. 17, details how the McClellan Committee discovered the various distortions of the Gorki letter.

33. "Labor Rackets—A Senate Feud?" *Newsweek* 50 (22 July 1958): 21-22; Mundt to Professor Kenneth Colgrove, 14 Dec. 1957, Mundt Papers, RG III, DB 701, Select Committee, FF 3, Karl E. Mundt Library, Madison, S.D.

34. Mundt Papers, RG III, DB 701, FF 3.

35. Schlesinger, *Kennedy*, 184; Mundt to "Ray" Moley, 5 June 1957, Mundt Papers, RG III, DB 701, FF 5; Kennedy, *Enemy Within*, 256.

36. Mundt Papers, RG III, DB 701, FF 3.

37. Mundt to McGovern, 3 Nov. 1958, ibid.; Schlesinger, *Kennedy*, 187; "Labor," *Fortune* 57 (Feb. 1957): 214; Kenneth P. O'Donnell and David F. Powers, *Johnnie, We Hardly Knew Ye* (New York: Pocket Books, 1973), 154.

38. Kennedy, *Enemy Within*, 260-66.

39. Mundt Papers, RG III, OB701, FF3; Kennedy, *Enemy Within*, 275-76.

40. Kennedy, *Enemy Within*, 276; Reuther to Goldwater, 7 March 1958, Reuther Papers, Box 113, Folder 2, WRPL; Goldwater to Reuther, 10 March 1958, ibid., Box 409, Folder 21.

41. John Barnard, *Walter Reuther and the Rise of the Auto Work-*

ers (Boston: Little, Brown, 1983), 165; Reuther, *Brothers Reuther*, 447. Mary McGrory wrote an editorial for the *Washington Star* emphasizing Reuther's stellar performance, clipping in Reuther Papers, Box 418, Folder 6, WPRL.

42. Kennedy, *Enemy Within*, 277-82; Mundt to Reuther, 22 April 1958, Mundt Papers, RG III, DB 705, FF 3; Reuther to Robert Kennedy, 2 January 1958, Reuther Papers, Box 113, File 1, WPRL; news story on McClellan's assessment in *Milwaukee Journal*, clipping in Reuther Papers, Box 418, File 6, WPRL.

43. Kennedy, *Enemy Within*, 284.

44. O'Donnell and Powers, *Johnnie*, 154-55.

45. *Senate Report 1417*, 86th Cong., 2d sess., Serial 12071, p. 450. The final report was *Senate Report 1139*, 86th Cong., 2d sess., Serial 12241.

46. Alan K. McAdams, *Power and Politics in Labor Legislation*, (New York: Columbia Univ. Press, 1964), 39-40, 48.

Chapter 4. Senator Kennedy Writes a Bill

1. Hutchinson, *Imperfect Union*, 154-64.

2. *Congress and the Nation* (Washington, D.C.: Congressional Quarterly Service, 1965), 604; *CR*, 85th Cong., 2d sess., p. 7054.

3. *CR*, 85th Cong., 2d sess., p. 7064.

4. William F. Knowland, "Why Not a Bill of Rights for Labor?" *Reader's Digest* 72 (May 1958): 79; *New York Times*, 23, 26, 27 April 1958; Telephone conversation between Lyndon Johnson and George Meany, 23 April 1958, LBJA, Container 57, LBJL.

5. Memorandum, George E. Reedy to Lyndon Johnson, 8 May 1958, Senate Papers, Container 428, LBJL.

6. *CR*, 85th Cong., 2d sess., pp. 7334-36.

7. Ibid., 7369-7512, 7524.

8. George Meany, Press conference, 6 Nov. 1958, p. 14, copy in Reuther Papers, Box 301, Folder 7, WPRL; McAdams, *Power and Politics*, 42-43; Copy of editorial, John Herling, "Hoffa's Legal Support," *Washington Daily News*, 25 June 1959, attached to letter from Paul Sifton to Walter Reuther, 26 June 1959, Reuther Papers, Box 422, Folder 3, WPRL.

9. *CR*, 85th Cong., 1 sess., pp. 17963-64, 18555; *Congress and the Nation*, 605. William J. Issacson, "Employee Welfare and Pension Plans: Regulation and Protection of Employee Rights," *Columbia Law Review* 59 (1959): 120-21, states that the House insisted on its version because congressmen believed the problem needed further

investigation, they feared a high cost of administering a more stringent law, and they did not trust the secretary of labor to administer
the tougher version.

10. *PPPUS, 1958,* 663-64.

11. James P. Mitchell to Robert W. Smith, n.d., James P. Mitchell
Papers, RG 174, Box 299, NA.

12. Walter Reuther to James Roosevelt, 2 June 1961, Reuther Papers, Box 412, Folder 20, WPRL; G. Robert Blakey, "Welfare and Pension Plans Disclosure Amendments of 1962," *Notre Dame Lawyer*
38 (April 1963): 270-86.

13. *PPPUS, 1958,* 118-24. The so-called no-man's-land came from
a case in 1957, *Guss* v. *Utah Labor Relations Board* (353 U.S. 1), in
which the Supreme Court held that federal law preempted state jurisdiction of the case based upon dollar amounts and created the nei-
ther/nor problem because the NLRB was not hearing such cases. The
NLRB had previously set an arbitrary amount for the size of cases it
would hear, based on dollar amounts, and before 1957 state courts
dealt with some of these smaller cases. After the *Guss* case, neither
level of government exerted jurisdiction. Management preferred the
more conservative state courts to have jurisdiction, but unions
wanted federal jurisdiction exercised. This was particularly a problem in the hotel and restaurant industries.

14. *Senate Report 1684,* 85th Cong., 2d sess., Serial 12062. Meany
later said that he was referring here to the "academics" who helped
write the Kennedy-Ives bill and that this was a turning point in his
relations with Kennedy. From then on, Kennedy would call Meany,
and "we got so that we could just discuss any of these things on a
straight forward basis" (George Meany Oral History Interview, p. 6,
JFKL).

15. Memorandum, George Reedy to Lyndon Johnson, 3 June
1958, Senate Papers, Box 428, LBJL.

16. Ibid., 5 June 1958.

17. Department of Labor Press Release, 9 June 1958, Gerald Morgan Papers, DDEL; Chronology of Labor Reform Legislation, Stuart
Rothman to the secretary of labor, 26 Aug. 1958, James Mitchell Papers, DDEL; George Reedy to Lyndon Johnson, 10 June 1958, Senate
Papers, Box 428, LBJL; *New York Times,* 10 June 1958.

18. *CR,* 85th Cong., 2d sess., pp. 10991, 11089.

19. Ibid., 11078-81.

20. Ibid., 11473; Chronology of Labor Reform Legislation, 1958,
p. 4, James Mitchell Papers, DDEL; McCabe interview.

21. This punitive legislation included Barden's, whose labor bill

in 1958 was described by Phil Landrum as "justifiably called a union-busting bill" (Landrum Oral History Interview, p. 2, JFKL). *CR*, 85th Cong., 2d sess., pp. 18275-76; Chronology of Labor Reform Legislation, 1958, p. 5, James Mitchell Papers, DDEL.

22. *CR*, 85th Cong., 2d sess., pp. 18266-68; Chronology of Labor Reform Legislation, 1958, p. 6, James Mitchell Papers, DDEL. When he heard rumors that the House might adjourn without voting on the Kennedy-Ives bill, John Kennedy met with the House Democratic leaders and persuaded them to vote on the measure, whether or not it passed (Frank Thompson Oral History Interview, p. 6-7, JFKL).

23. Telegram in LBJA, Container 7, LBJL; *CR*, 85th Cong., 2d sess., pp. 18275-76.

24. *CR*, 85th Cong., 2d sess., pp. 18268-69, 18266.

25. Ibid., 18287-88; Memorandum, Reedy to Johnson, n.d., Senate Papers, LBJL.

26. *New York Times*, 21, 24, 19 Aug. 1958.

27. Sam Rayburn to Gerald S. Chargin, 25 Aug. 1958, SRL; Memorandum on Kennedy-Ives bill, 21 Aug. 1958, Mitchell Papers, DDEL.

28. *PPPUS, 1958*, 663, 778; *Newsweek* 52 (4 Aug. 1958): 11 and (11 Aug. 1958): 15-16.

29. *New York Times*, 18 Aug. 1958.

30. Memorandum, Reedy to Johnson, 29 July 1958, Senate Papers, Box 428, LBJL.

31. R. Alton Lee, "Federal Assistance to Depressed Areas in the Postwar Recessions," *Western Economic Journal* 1 (Fall 1963): 19-21. Edward W. Chester, "1958: The Economic Recession and Right to Work," chap. 4 of his forthcoming *The Kaleidoscope of Politics: Midterm Elections since 1946*, concludes that these two issues dominated these elections. I am grateful to Professor Chester for allowing me to read this chapter.

32. *Newsweek* 52 (10 Nov. 1958): 44; *U.S. News & World Report* 45 (14 Nov. 1958): 47; Totten J. Anderson, "The 1958 Election in California," *Western Political Quarterly* 12 (March 1959): 276. See also Ross R. Rice, "The 1958 Election in Arizona," in ibid., 266-75.

33. *New Republic* 139 (1 Dec. 1958): 6; the "plot" against Goldwater is in the *New York Times*, 5 Nov. 1958. See also Rice, "The 1958 Election in Arizona," 271.

34. Walter P. Reuther to Chester Bowles, 21 Jan. 1959, Reuther Papers, Box 412, Folder 6, WPRL; Chester, "1958," 9-10.

35. Hutchinson, *Imperfect Union*, 361; *Newsweek* 52 (17 Nov. 1958): 30.
36. Lee, *Eisenhower*, 287-89; *Time* 73 (6 April 1959): 18, 19.
37. *Time* 73 (19 Jan. 1959): 16.
38. *Newsweek* 53 (19 Jan. 1959): 20; David B. Truman, *The Congressional Party* (New York: Wiley, 1959), 208.

Chapter 5. Senator Kennedy Tries Again

1. Dr. George H. Gallup, *The Gallup Poll* (New York: Random House, 1972), 1591.
2. *Atlantic* 203 (March 1959): 12; McAdams, *Power and Politics*, 58, 86.
3. Edward Onanian, "Title VII of the Landrum-Griffin Act: The Taft-Hartley Amendments" (Ph.D. dissertation, Univ. of Illinois, 1963), 37-39; *New York Times*, 19 Feb. 1969.
4. James P. Mitchell to the president, 18 Feb. 1959, James P. Mitchell Papers, RG 174, Box 305, NA.
5. *PPPUS, 1959*, 143-46.
6. *U.S. News & World Report* 46 (6 Feb. 1959): 96; McCabe interview. McCabe noted in a White House memo that "about once every ten years Congress screws up its courage and passes some kind of a labor bill" (Edward A. McCabe to Bob Gray, 6 April 1959, OF 124, Box 631, Eisenhower Papers, DDEL).
7. McAdams, *Power and Politics*, 59-60.
8. Ibid., 58-59.
9. *Newsweek* 53 (16 Feb. 1959): 25.
10. Memorandum, Reedy to Johnson, 26 March 1959, Senate Papers, Box 429, LBJL; Oral History, George Reedy, 4:32, LBJL.
11. Memorandum, Reedy to Johnson, 3 March 1959, Senate Papers, Box 429, LBJL.
12. 24 March 1959, Legislative Meeting Series, Ann Whitman File, DDEL. The story of Johnson and Dirksen agreeing to wait for House action is in *Newsweek* 53 (16 March 1959): 26.
13. James P. Mitchell to Barry Goldwater, 10 April 1959, RG 174, Box 305, NA.
14. *Senate Report 187*, 86th Cong., 1st sess., Serial 12149, p.7.
15. Ibid., 117.
16. Memorandum, Edward A. McCabe to Bob Gray, 6 April 1959, OF 124, Eisenhower Papers, DDEL.
17. *CR*, 86th Cong., 1st sess., pp. 5985, 6411.
18. *New York Times*, 23 April 1959. As early as 1947, when Con-

gress debated the Taft-Hartley Act, the American Civil Liberties Union and Fred Hartley had unsuccessfully urged a workers' bill of rights. See Doris B. McLaughlin and Anita W. Schoomaker, *The Landrum-Griffin Act and Union Democracy* (Ann Arbor: Univ. of Michigan Press, 1979), 74.

19. *CR*, 86th Cong., 1st sess., pp. 6492-93; McAdams, *Power and Politics*, 95-97.

20. *Newsweek* 53 (4 May 1959): 26; George Reedy, Oral History, 15:3, LBJL.

21. Edward Joseph Hickey, Jr., "The Bill of Rights of Union Members," *Georgetown Law Journal* 48 (Winter 1959): 232; *New York Times*, 8, 11 May 1959; McAdams, *Power and Politics*, 98-101.

22. *Reporter* 20 (14 May 1959): 4; Memorandum, unsigned, undated, Senate Papers, LBJL; McAdams, *Power and Politics*, 101-4.

23. *CR*, 86th Cong., 1st sess., pp. 6680, 6671. See McAdams, *Power and Politics*, 104-6, for the changing mood of the country and Congress.

24. McAdams, *Power and Politics*, 106-12.

25. *CR*, 86th Cong., 1st sess., p. 6745. Senator Goldwater was pleased when the conference committee on Landrum-Griffin included "practically every amendment" he had offered in the final law (Barry Goldwater to the author, 4 Feb. 1988).

26. The "frenzied lawyers" quote is from a Foreword by Joseph A. Loftus to a series of articles on the Landrum-Griffin Act in *Georgetown Law Journal* 48 (Winter 1959): 207.

27. Memorandum, Edward A. McCabe to Jerry Morgan, 1 June 1959, McCabe Papers, DDEL.

Chapter 6. The Two Sides Gird for Battle

1. C. Douglas Dorough, *Mr. Sam* (New York: Random House, 1962), 537-38.

2. *New York Times*, 21-22 May 1959.

3. Several news journals carried stories about these breakfasts: *Time* 74 (27 July 1959): 12-13; *Life* 47 (27 July 1959): 30; *Newsweek* 54 (18 May 1959): 31, 32. The Halleck quote is in the *New York Times*, 28 May 1959.

4. *Newsweek* 53 (1 June 1959): 21.

5. McCabe interview.

6. McAdams, *Power and Politics*, 120, 158-59. The undersecretary of labor sent Mitchell a copy of the Small Business Men's Association letter with the notation, "part of our program, I'm told, to

promote a sound labor reform bill" (Albert L. McDermott to the secretary of labor, 29 July 1959, Mitchell Papers, Box 305, NA).

7. McCabe interview; *Newsweek* 53 (6 April 1959): 27.

8. *Time* 73 (8 June 1959), 15-18 has an interesting article on Halleck and his leadership, describing his party leadership as "stricter than any time" since "Uncle Joe" Cannon.

9. McCabe interview.

10. Author's interview with Robert P. Griffin, 20 June 1985, hereafter cited as Griffin interview. The quote is from Henry Z. Scheele, *Charlie Halleck* (New York: Exposition Press, 1966), 189.

11. Phil M. Landrum, Sr., to the author, 8 Aug. 1985.

12. McAdams, *Power and Politics*, 142-43.

13. Richard Bolling, *House Out of Order* (New York: Dutton, 1965), 165-66.

14. McAdams, *Power and Politics*, 132.

15. Ibid., 144-48; Bolling, *House*, 166. Udall recalled that, in vain, House leaders continued to tell AFL-CIO leaders that "they were erroneous in their assumption that you could take a bill to the floor of the House at that time that had a labor label—and get a majority" (Stewart Udall Oral History Interview, p. 13, JFKL).

16. *Life* 47 (27 July 1959): 30; *Time* 74 (27 July 1959): 12-13.

17. Harold N. Nystrom to secretary of labor, 18 July 1959, Mitchell Papers, RG 174, Box 302, NA; Legislative meeting, 21 July 1959, Legislative Meeting Series, Ann Whitman File, DDEL.

18. *Time* 74 (3 Aug. 1959): 18; *New York Times*, 24 July 1959.

19. *House Report 741*, 86th Cong., 1st sess., Serial 12162.

20. Speaker Rayburn's Comments on Proposed Labor Legislation, 3 Aug. 1959, SRL.

21. Ruth Hagy's College News Conference, 26 July 1959, Everett M. Dirksen Papers, Remarks and Releases, Dirksen Congressional Center, Pekin, Illinois.

22. McCabe interview; McAdams, *Power and Politics*, 175-76; Scheel, *Halleck*, 188-89.

23. *New York Times*, 30 July 1959.

24. Ibid.; Ten Congressmen to the President, 31 July 1959, OF 99, Eisenhower Papers, DDEL; McAdams, *Power and Politics*, 178.

25. Undated memorandum, Senate Papers, LBJL. Landrum agreed there was "not a great deal of difference" between the two proposals in the first six titles (Landrum Oral History Interview, p. 6, JFKL).

26. Ibid McCabe interview.

27. Bolling, *House*, 167-68.

28. McCabe interview.

29. *U.S. News & World Report* 47 (10 Aug. 1959): 89. Congressman James Fulton of Pennsylvania telegraphed the Kennedy brothers that 60 percent of his "heavy mail" was in response to Robert's TV appearance and all "want immediate passage of corrective legislation" (Telegram, 27 July 1959, John F. Kennedy, Pre-Presidential Papers, Box 722, JFKL).

30. *Newsweek* 54 (10 Aug. 1959): 20; *Time* 74 (17 Aug. 1959): 19.

31. McCabe interview.

32. *PPPUS, 1959*, 567-71.

33. *Newsweek* 54 (10 Aug. 1959): 20; Griffin interview; Landrum to the author, 8 Aug. 1985; McAdams, *Power and Politics*, 196. Senator Richard Russell of Georgia, for example, received 650 letters and telegrams in favor of the Landrum-Griffin bill and only 25 in opposition to it (William H. Jordan to Senator Russell, 19 Aug. 1959, Richard B. Russell Papers, Russell Library, University of Georgia, Athens).

34. Address of the Honorable Sam Rayburn, 10 Aug. 1959, copy in SRL; Bolling, *House*, 169.

35. *New York Times*, 9 Aug. 1959.

Chapter 7. The Forces Engage

1. *New York Times*, 6, 20 Aug. 1959; *Time* 74 (17 Aug. 1959): 20.

2. Bolling, *House*, 168.

3. Ibid., 169; McAdams, *Power and Politics*, 204.

4. *CR*, 86th Cong., 1st sess., p. 15512.

5. Bolling, *House*, 170.

6. McAdams, *Power and Politics*, 210.

7. *New York Times*, 5, 13 Aug. 1959.

8. Legislative Meeting Series, 28 July 1959 and 11 Aug. 1959, Ann Whitman File, DDEL.

9. *U.S. News & World Report* 47 (24 Aug. 1959): 34; *Time* 74 (24 Aug. 1959): 13.

10. McAdams, *Power and Politics*, 211-15; McCabe interview; Griffin interview; Bruce J. Dierenenfield, *Keeper of the Rules: Congressman Howard W. Smith of Virginia* (Charlottesville: Univ. Press of Virginia, 1987), 168.

11. McAdams, *Power and Politics*, 217-20.

12. Bolling, *House*, 170; *CR*, 86th Cong., 1st sess., pp. 15722, 15728.

13. McAdams, *Power and Politics*, 224-25.

14. *CR,* 86th Cong., 1st sess., p. 15834; McCabe interview.

15. The "six Republicans" quote is from McAdams, *Power and Politics,* 228; *CR,* 86th Cong., 1st sess., pp. 15848, 15853, 15858; Walker, "Hoffman," 319.

16. Scheele, *Halleck,* 190.

17. Telephone interview with Kenneth McGuiness, 18 Feb. 1987.

18. *New York Times,* 17 Aug. 1959, reported that on 7 December 1931 the House set a record in voting for a Speaker. John Nance Garner received 218 votes, Bertrand Snell 207, George Schneider 5, and 3 voted "present."

19. Mundt to Barden, 17 Aug. 1959, Mundt Papers.

20. Alfred E. Santangelo, "The Passage of LMRDA and Economic Motivations," in Solenko, *Symposium on the Labor-Management Reporting and Disclosure Act of 1959,* 88-89.

21. Richard Bolling interview, 1 Nov. 1965, p. 14, copy in SRL; Bolling, *House,* 172; Landrum to the author, 8 Aug. 1985.

22. McAdams, *Power and Politics,* 235-36; *Newsweek* 54 (24 Aug. 1959): 17.

23. McAdams, *Power and Politics,* 240; McCabe interview; Karl E. Mundt, "Dear Friend" letter to constituents, 21 Aug. 1959, Mundt Papers.

24. McCabe interview.

25. A copy of this letter is in the Dirksen Papers, Dirksen Congressional Center.

26. Lyndon Johnson, "Dear Friend" letter to constituents, 15 Aug. 1959, Senate Papers; Memorandum, George Reedy to Senator Johnson, 9 Nov. 1959, Senate Papers, Box 43, LBJL.

27. Telephone interview with Kenneth McGuiness, 18 Feb. 1987. McGuiness reported that the secondary boycott issue was settled at one of these dinners.

28. Decisions in the conference are from working papers of Senator Dirksen, Dirksen Congressional Center, unless otherwise noted.

29. Intraoffice file, II, Box 22, Aug. 1959, Richard B. Russell Papers.

30. *Newsweek* 54 (14 Sept. 1959): 29, 48; McCabe interview; McAdams, *Power and Politics,* 258-59.

31. Robert Griffin reported that David Dubinsky was putting great pressure on John Kennedy to exempt the garment workers and the senator yielded because he wanted the large number of votes Dubinsky would bring to the Democratic national convention that next year (Griffin interview).

32. McAdams, *Power and Politics,* 260-61.

33. Memorandum, George Reedy to Senator Johnson, n.d., Senate Papers, Box 43, LBJL.

34. *CR*, 86th Cong., 1st sess., pp. 17919, 18153-54.

35. The value-laden terms *secondary boycott* and *hot cargo* are not used in the law. Instead, it prohibits "inducement of individuals" or "threaten, coerce, or restrain an individual." See David Previant, "The New Hot Cargo and Secondary Boycott Sections: A Critical Analysis," *Georgetown Law Journal* 48 (Winter 1959): 346.

36. It was often overlooked at the time, and later, that the Rackets Committee revelations of management corruption brought some reform in that category of labor-management relations. See Guy Farmer and N. Thompson Powers, "The Employer Reporting Requirements and Section 302 of Taft-Hartley as Amended," *Northwestern Law Review* 54 (Jan.-Feb. 1960): 782.

37. Memorandum for the president, 12 Sept. 1959, Bill File on S. 1555, DDEL. In an interview, Edward McCabe stressed that the language of the Landrum-Griffin Act closely followed what the president had requested. The law prohibited communists and felons from holding office or serving as labor relations consultants in a union.

38. Wayne Morse to Walter Reuther, 13 Oct. 1969, Reuther Papers, Box 411, Folder 69, WPRL. Senator Goldwater believed that Kennedy "didn't have a lot to do with the conference" because it "was completely handled by Senator Dirksen and between he [*sic*], and the friends in the House, we have a bill that's not too bad" (Goldwater to the author, 4 Feb. 1988). Kennedy's form letter response to constituents who congratulated him on the final bill described the Landrum-Griffin Act as "sound and in the public interest" (John F. Kennedy, Pre-Presidential Papers, Box 722, JFKL).

39. George Reedy Oral History, 15:20-21, LBJL; Archibald Cox, "The Landrum-Griffin Amendments to the National Labor Relations Act," *Minnesota Law Review* 44 (Dec. 1959): 260.

Chapter 8. The Impact of the Law

1. McLaughlin and Schoomaker, *Landrum-Griffin*, 2.

2. Frank M. Keiler, "The Impact of Titles I-VI of the Landrum-Griffin Act," *Georgia Law Review* 3 (Winter 1969): 379.

3. Janice R. Bellace and Alan D. Berkowitz, *The Landrum-Griffin Act: Twenty Years of Federal Protection of Union Members' Rights* (Philadelphia: Univ. of Pennsylvania Press, 1981), 95-97, 308-11.

4. McLaughlin and Schoomaker, *Landrum-Griffin*, 130-31, 139-

43, 149; the quote is from Bellace and Berkowitz, *Landrum-Griffin*, 149.

5. Bellace and Berkowitz, *Landrum-Griffin*, 280-82; the quote is from Robert L. Bircham, "Labor Democracy in America: The Impact of Titles I and IV of the Landrum-Griffin Act," *Villanova Law Review* 13 (Fall 1967): 56.

6. Joseph L. Rauh, Jr., "LMDRA—Enforce It or Repeal It," *Georgia Law Review* 5 (Summer 1971): 643-51. *Newsweek* 75 (2 Feb. 1970): 22 carried a story of the arrests for murder.

7. Robert P. Griffin, "The Landrum-Griffin Act: Twelve Years of Experience in Protecting Employee Rights," *Georgia Law Review* 5 (Summer 1971): 642.

8. McLaughlin and Schoomaker, *Landrum-Griffin*, 181-86.

9. Ibid., 179.

10. Philip Taft, "The Impact of Landrum-Griffin on Union Government," *Annals of the American Academy of Political and Social Science* 333 (Jan. 1961): 136, 140.

11. *Newsweek* 109 (22 June 1987): 43.

12. Onanian, "Title VII," 170-73, 177; Edward B. Shils, "Impact of Landrum-Griffin on the Small Employer," *Annals of the American Academy of Political and Social Science* 333 (Jan. 1961): 152. On the Teamsters, see Estelle James, "Jimmy Hoffa: Labor Hero or Labor's Own Foe?" in Melvyn Dubofsky and Warren Van Tine, eds., *Labor Leaders in America* (Urbana: Univ. of Illinois Press, 1987), 312-13. Michael Goldfield, *The Decline of Organized Labor in the United States* (Chicago: Univ. of Chicago Press, 1987), 184, 225-26, argues that this is one of the three primary reasons for union decline, the others being an increased employer resistance and less aggressiveness in union organizing.

13. Onanian, "Title VII," 179-81.

14. Ibid., 183-84.

15. Ibid., 184.

16. Ibid., 185.

17. Ibid.

Chapter 9. Some Assessments

1. Robinson, *George Meany*, 208n.; see also Joseph C. Goulden, *Meany* (New York: Atheneum, 1972), 228-29.

2. Loftus, "LMRDA in Retrospect," 10.

3. Dorough, *Mr. Sam*, 9-12.

4. Donald R. Anderson, "The Trusteeship Imbroglio," *Yale Law Journal* 71 (July 1962): 1520-21.

5. McGuiness interview; Jesse I. Etelson and Franklin N. Smith, Jr., "Union Discipline under the Landrum-Griffin Act," *Harvard Law Review* 82 (Feb. 1969): 771.

6. Robert P. Griffin, "A New Era in Labor-Management Relations," in Slovenko, *Symposium on the Labor-Management Reporting and Disclosure Act of 1959*, 30.

Index